CARMELITE BIBLE MEDITATIONS

The Sound of Silen(

Listening to the Word of God with Elijah t(

BY JOSEPH CHALMERS, O.CARM.

THE SOUND OF SILENCE

*Listening to the Word of God
with Elijah the Prophet*

BY JOSEPH CHALMERS, O.CARM.

Saint Albert's Press & Edizioni Carmelitane
2007

First published 2007 by Saint Albert's Press & Edizioni Carmelitane.

Saint Albert's Press
Whitefriars, 35 Tanners Street,
Faversham, Kent, ME13 7JN, United Kingdom
www.carmelite.org
ISBN-10: 0-904849-34-1
ISBN-13: 978-0-904849-34-9

Edizioni Carmelitane
Centro Internationale S. Alberto
Via Sforza Pallavicini, 10
00193 Roma, Italy
www.carmelites.info/edizioni
ISBN-13: 978-88-7288-100-2

Edited and designed by Johan Bergström-Allen, Carmelite Projects & Publications Office, York.

Typeset by Jakub Kubů, Praha, Czech Republic.
Printed by ERMAT Praha, s.r.o., Czech Republic.
Production coordinated by Pavel Kindermann on behalf of Karmelitánské nakladatelství, s.r.o.,
Kostelní Vydří 58, 380 01 Dačice, Czech Republic, www.kna.cz.

CONTENTS

ILLUSTRATIONS

It is sometimes said that the saints are like windows who allow the light of God to shine through them. For this reason the illustrations chosen for this book are stained glass windows associated with Elijah and his disciple Elisha.

Saint Albert's Press is grateful to the individuals, communities and churches which have allowed us to reproduce their artworks.

Page 96: The prophet Elijah encouraged by an angel. Window by Marc Chagall. Stefanskirche, Mainz, Germany. Photograph by Riccardo Palazzi, O.Carm.

Pages 102: The prophet Elijah bearing his name on a scroll. Window in St. Edward the Confessor Church, Dringhouses, York, produced by Wailes of Newcastle. Photograph by Johan Bergström-Allen.

Page 110: The prophet Elisha. Window by Richard Joseph King at the National Shrine of Saint Jude, Whitefriars, Faversham Kent, England. © British Province of Carmelites. Photograph by Johan Bergström-Allen.

Page 116: Elisha depicted in a medieval stained glass 'Tree of Jesse' window (c.1340) in the Church of Saint Mary in Shrewsbury, in the care of the Churches Conservation Trust. Photograph by Johan Bergström-Allen.

Page 122: The prophet Elijah. Window in the chapel of the National Shrine of Saint Thérèse in Darien, Illinois, U.S.A. © Carmelite Province of the Most Pure Heart of Mary. Photograph by Johan Bergström-Allen.

Page 128: Rays of light shining from Christ upon the prophet Elisha (Elijah). Window at St. Michael and All Angels Anglican Church, Winnipeg, Manitoba, Canada. Photograph by Steven Thiessen.

Page 134: The ascent of Elijah. Window (1863) by Lavers & Barraud, originally in Trinity Methodist Church, Wolverhampton, Staffordshire, now in The Stained Glass Museum, Ely, Cambridgeshire. Gift of the Minister and Congregation, 1976. © The Stained Glass Museum, Ely. Photograph by Susan Mathews.

Page 142: The prophet Elijah rising to paradise in a fiery charity. Window by Marianne Behle-Downs, completed by McNicholas Studios, Warwick, New York, in Christ Church, Pompton Lakes, New Jersey. Photograph by John Rollins.

Page 148: Christ, Virgin Mary and Holy Spirit on Carmel. Window by George Walsh in the Chapel of Avila Discalced Carmelite Friary, Morehampton Road, Dublin, Ireland. © Anglo-Irish Province of Discalced Carmelites. Photograph by Johan Bergström-Allen.

FOREWORD

This book began life in Italian and I wrote it at the request of a fellow Carmelite friar, Fr. Bruno Secondin, O.Carm., the renowned theologian of the spiritual life.[1] For several years he has conducted a bi-monthly *Lectio Divina* Bible meditation session in the Carmelite church of Traspontina, very close to Saint Peter's Basilica in Rome. This is a very popular event not least because of the famous people who, from time to time, lead the *Lectio Divina*. A few years ago a certain Cardinal Joseph Ratzinger (now Pope Benedict XVI) directed the session.

Several books have emerged from these sessions. I have also had an interest in the prophet Elijah for a long time and so decided to write a book for prayer using the texts regarding Elijah. While waiting for it to be published I decided to translate it into English. While doing so I took the opportunity to change certain parts, add, subtract and hopefully make the whole book a little better.

I hope that you might find what I have written of some help. My suggestion is that rather than reading the whole book through at once you might take each reflection individually, perhaps over the course of a fortnight.

We are all companions on the spiritual journey into the mystery of God. Those who have gone before us can help us by their prayers and their example. With the help of the prophet Elijah, let us listen to the sound of silence wherein God speaks. The Word of God is something alive and active (*Hebrews* 4:12). The following words from the *Letter to the Hebrews* could be understood as referring also to the Prophet Elijah:

> Remember your leaders, who preached the word of God to you, and as you reflect on the outcome of their lives, take their faith as your model. (13:7)

Joseph Chalmers, O.Carm.
Rome

---

1   The original Italian edition was *Il Suono Del Silenzio: Ascoltando La Parola di Dio con il Profeta Elia*, (Edizioni Messaggero Padova, 2006).

INTRODUCTION

Christian prayer involves communication with God, being in relationship with God. There are many ways of prayer and many models for prayer. One of the ancient ways of prayer that has witnessed a resurgence in recent years is *Lectio Divina*, which is the prayerful reading of Holy Scripture, the Bible.[2] All prayer in theory should be open to and should encourage the flowering of contemplation, which is a loving, intimate knowledge of God that is a completely gratuitous divine gift.

When seeking to plumb the depths of the Scriptures, it is appropriate to look for help to the great heroes of our faith, the saints, and particularly to the major figures of the Bible. In this book I have chosen to take the prophet Elijah (sometimes called Elias) as guide. We will enter into the stories that were told of him and passed on from generation to generation in oral form for hundreds of years before they were ever written down. We will try to discover what God is saying to us today through these fascinating stories of the hero of ancient Israel.

Why choose a prophet, who is so distant from us, to help us on our journey of prayer? What can a person who comes from a culture and a time so different from ours tell us about prayer?

The Church sees in the prophet Elijah a model for prayer. The 1992 *Catechism of the Catholic Church* in fact says the following:

> **2582** Elijah is the "father" of the prophets, "the generation of those who seek him, who seek the face of the God of Jacob." Elijah's name, "The Lord is my God," foretells the people's cry in response to his prayer on Mount Carmel. Saint James refers to Elijah in order to encourage us to pray: "The prayer of the righteous is powerful and effective."

> **2583** After Elijah had learned mercy during his retreat at the Wadi Cherith, he teaches the widow of Zarephath to believe in the Word of God and confirms her faith by his urgent prayer: God brings the widow's child back to life.

> The sacrifice on Mount Carmel is a decisive test for the faith of the People of God. In response to Elijah's plea, "Answer me, O LORD,

---

2   There are very many books about the theory and history of *Lectio Divina*. Two of the best introductions in English are Thelma Hall, *Too Deep For Words* (New York: Paulist Press, 1988) and Michael Casey, *Sacred Reading* (Liguori, Missouri: Triumph Books, 1996).

answer me," the Lord's fire consumes the holocaust, at the time of the evening oblation. The Eastern liturgies repeat Elijah's plea in the Eucharistic *epiclesis*.

Finally, taking the desert road that leads to the place where the living and true God reveals himself to his people, Elijah, like Moses before him, hides "in a cleft of the rock" until the mysterious presence of God has passed by. But only on the mountain of the Transfiguration will Moses and Elijah behold the unveiled face of him whom they sought; "the light of the knowledge of the glory of God [shines] in the face of Christ," crucified and risen.

2584 In their "one to one" encounters with God, the prophets draw light and strength for their mission. Their prayer is not flight from this unfaithful world, but rather attentiveness to the Word of God. At times their prayer is an argument or a complaint, but it is always an intercession that awaits and prepares for the intervention of the Saviour God, the Lord of history.

The importance of the prophet Elijah

In the history of Israel, the prophet Elijah is on the same level as Moses, one of the greatest of the earliest prophets of the Old Testament. The Jewish people still wait for Elijah's return as the precursor of the Messiah, and at the Passover meal they lay a place for him at table. Several times the Gospel accounts refer to him in relation to John the Baptist. On Mount Tabor, Elijah appeared alongside Moses speaking with Jesus (*Matthew* 17:1-8; *Mark* 9:2-8; *Luke* 9:28-36). The figure of the prophet Elijah is common not only to Christians and Jews but also to Muslims because although not a major figure, he does appear in the Koran as a prophet.

The Carmelite Order – one of the ancient religious orders of the Roman Catholic Church – takes it name from Mount Carmel in the Holy Land. Mount Carmel is remembered as the site of a contest which took place between Elijah, the prophet of the true God, and the prophets of Baal, a false god. The first Carmelite hermits gathered around a spring called the Well of Elijah sometime at the beginning of the thirteenth century, and no doubt the memory of the prophet of Carmel was important for these men.

In Carmelite spirituality the prophet Elijah is still recognised as an inspirational model for today. Carmelites stress that from the prophet Elijah they learn to have an undivided heart, dedicated to the service of God. They see in him a man who made a choice without compromise for the cause of God. Carmelites also see in the prophet a channel of God's tenderness towards the poor.[3]

In the document used to teach young Carmelites about the importance of the prophet Elijah for the Order, we find the following:

> Some pilgrims, coming from the West to the Holy Land, chose Mount Carmel as the place in which to live as hermits in community. They settled near the spring known as 'Elijah's spring', thus continuing a long tradition of monastic and eremitic presence.
>
> The memory of the prophet is still alive in this place: the prophet burning with zeal for his God, whose word is a flaming torch; the prophet who stands in God's presence, ever ready to serve him and to obey his Word; the prophet who points to the true God so that the people may no longer stand with their feet in two camps; the prophet who exhorts his people to choose to focus their existence on God alone; the prophet who is attentive both to the voice of God and to the cry of the poor, who knows how to defend both the rights of the one God and those of God's beloved ones, the weakest and the last.
>
> Carmelites remember, and in some ways relive, the prophet's experience. He hid in the desert in times of dryness and faced the challenge of the false prophets of a dead idol, which was incapable of giving life. He journeyed back through the desert to Mount Horeb, to meet the Lord in new and unexpected ways, and to understand that God is present even where he appears to be absent. Carmelites share in Elijah's thirst for justice and know themselves to be, like Elisha, heirs to the mantle that fell from heaven, from the chariot engulfed in flames.[4]

---

3   When the Carmelites arrived in Europe from Mount Carmel in the 13th Century they began to construct a mythical history of the Order and looked to the prophet Elijah as founder. The most famous of these "histories" was written in Latin in the late 14th century by the Carmelite friar Felip Ribot. We now have a translation of this whole work into English by Richard Copsey, *The Ten Books on the Way of Life and Great Deeds of the Carmelites*, (Faversham & Rome: Saint Albert's Press & Edizioni Carmelitane, 2005). For a modern approach to the importance of the prophet Elijah in Carmelite spirituality, see: Peter Slattery, *The Springs of Carmel*, (New York: St. Paul's, 1991, reprinted by Alba House, 2000); Wilfrid McGreal, *At the Fountain of Elijah: the Carmelite Tradition*, (London: Darton, Longman & Todd, 1999); Jane Ackerman, *Elijah: Prophet of Carmel*, (Washington D.C.: ICS Publications, 2003); James McCaffery, 'The Heritage of Elijah' in *The Carmelite Charism: Exploring the Biblical Roots*, (Dublin: Veritas Publications, 2004); Kevin Alban, (ed.), *Journeying with Carmel: Extracts from the 1995 Carmelite Constitutions*, (Middle Park, Victoria: Carmelite Communications, 1997), p.19.

4   *Carmelite Formation: A Journey of Transformation - Ratio Institutionis Vitæ Carmelitanæ*, (Rome: General Curia of the Carmelite Order, 2000), no. 46.

The context of the prophet Elijah

After his time on earth this austere prophet remained alive in the people's memory to the point that there arose dramatic and miraculous stories about him. From the end of the 9th century before Christ there could be found a series of stories concerning Elijah. Shortly afterwards the stories concerning Elijah's disciple Elisha (sometimes called Eliseus) came about. These can all be found in the Bible in the so-called *Elijah saga cycle* (*1 Kings* 17 - *2 Kings* 1) and in the tales of Elisha (*2 Kings* 2-13).

The prophet Elijah lived at the time of King Ahab (874-853 B.C.) who was son of Omri (885-874 B.C.). Omri, who was an army general, took power in a coup-d'état against King Zimri (886-885 B.C.). He was the sixth king of Israel in forty-six years, after the separation from Judah, which came about in the year 931 B.C. in the reign of King Jeroboam I. Omri began the fourth dynasty and founded the fourth capital (Sichem, Penuel, Tirsa and Samaria). There was great instability at this time. His reign lasted twelve years and it began a time of peace and an economic upswing, which was continued in the reign of his son, Ahab. Despite these positive elements, the Bible has very little to say about Omri. The aim of Omri's politics was to bring stability to the country and to increase its economic power.

The stories about Elijah were conserved and spread above all during the great Exile, when the people of Israel found themselves in a situation without hope, seemingly abandoned. They lived daily with frustration, destruction and in a state of utter confusion. Several times the people of Israel had suffered deportation after defeat in war. However, the deportation to Babylonia left a lasting and profound impact on the soul of the people. It seemed that God had renounced the plan of salvation whereby God had brought the people out of the slavery of Egypt into the Promised Land. After the deportations, many believed that the situation would only last a short while, but that was an illusion. The stories about the *prophet of fire* helped the exiles to understand something of their situation, notwithstanding the official attempts to interpret events in a totally different way.[5]

On returning from exile, the people began to speak of the ancient prophets as those who had given them hope, and in a particular way, this hope centred on the prophet Elijah. Several times he is written of in Scripture outside the stories

---

5   *Prophet of Fire* is the title of an excellent little study on the implications of the prophet Elijah for Carmelite spirituality by the former Prior General of the Order, Kilian Healy (Rome: Institutum Carmelitanum, 1990), reprinted in 2004 as volume 5 in the *Carmel in the World Paperbacks* series.

that appear in the *Books of the Kings*. I list these texts in Appendix II at the back of this book.

The context of the life of the prophet Elijah is the struggle within Israel against religious syncretism, a mixing of two religions, taking the values and divine attributes present in one religion and confusing them with those of another religion. Yahweh, God of the Israelites, had brought the people out of Egypt and had guided them to the Promised Land. Yahweh was a jealous God: "You shall have no other gods before me" (*Deuteronomy* 5:7). At the time of Elijah, paganism was profoundly rooted among the simple people. They honoured God with the name of the Lord Yahweh, but in reality the one they worshipped was in fact the pagan deity, Baal. The name we give to God is not as important as the ideas that this name evokes. It seems also that the people followed pagan practices, for example child sacrifice and ritual prostitution in places sacred to idols.

We know very little about Elijah as a person. Probably the basis of the stories about Elijah comes from a source containing his life and works, but the final editor of the *Books of the Kings* used only a part of this document, and he does not seem to be interested in the biographical details of the prophet. It is clear that the final text is the result of a development of a tradition in which the most ancient stories about Elijah were adapted by successive generations when they had to confront new problems and new situations. The sources used for the *Books of the Kings* are numerous. In the Hebrew Bible the two *Books of the Kings* form a unity. Greek translators separated them in the third century before Christ. In these books we do not find a scientific history, but a theological vision of history. This means that the facts are presented according to what the author thinks about God and the relationship between God and the people. The author wants to teach his readers something about God and is not interested in the ordinary facts of history. The interest of the *Books of the Kings* is in the monarchy in general and in its failures. The author wants to underline that the kings were not faithful to God and that many problems arose from this fact.

In the cycle of Elijah stories one can distinguish three blocks: *1 Kings* 17-19; *1 Kings* 21; and *2 Kings* 1. The account of the assumption of Elijah to heaven in a chariot of fire (his death) in *2 Kings* 2 and, according to some scholars, also the vocation of Elisha (*1 Kings* 19:19-21) do not properly speaking form part of the Elijah saga cycle, but to that of Elisha. The story of Naboth in *1 Kings* 21 and that of Acaziah in *2 Kings* 1 seem to be isolated, while the rest of the stories, which can be found in *1 Kings* 17-19, are developed as a continuous story with a structure and some themes that give a literary unity to these stories.

From the thematic point of view, the block of stories in chapters 17-19 of the *First Book of Kings* forms a unity on two levels. Above all it is the religious history of the prophet from his first public appearance and his activity in the struggle against religious syncretism to the appointment of Elisha as his successor. In this context the account of the persecution of the prophet is inserted. This is the theme that unifies the whole structure and is present from the beginning vaguely (cf. 17:3), and then more evidently (cf. 18:4 ff.) and finally in an explicit fashion (cf. 19:1 ff.). The other element that unites the whole cycle is the treatment of Elijah as a Moses figure: Elijah is presented as the new Moses. There is also the great conflict between two religions: Yahwism and Baalism, represented respectively by Elijah and by Jezebel, her prophets and also Ahab. This is evident in chapter 18, but is present in substance throughout the whole Elijan cycle.

A mysterious person

In these stories we meet a man who kept the religion of Israel alive. Elijah was totally available for God. He stood before God like a servant awaiting instructions (*1 Kings* 17:1; 18:15, 36). Like all the prophets, he was completely grasped by the Word of God. We could say that the subject of the cycle of the stories about Elijah is really not the prophet but God, whose Word was not only the motive for reflection in the silence and solitude, but also a fire to burn out evil from the human heart. Elijah's total openness to the Word of God led him to live a very particular style of life. Elijah wanted to be a visible sign in Israel, a sign that challenged the complacent attitudes of the people. The prophet did not go along with the opinions of his day, but he was prepared to stand out so that his entire life would be an open criticism of the values of the people. A prophet can only be a sign for others if he himself, first of all, allows himself to be grasped by God. Elijah was a man of mystery, known for his sudden appearances and disappearances (*1 Kings* 18:12). His final disappearance in the chariot of fire left an enduring impression in Israel (*2 Kings* 2:11).

The two principal characteristics of Elijah are his faithfulness and his creativity. He was totally faithful to his religious traditions, and was the champion of fidelity to the covenant that God had made with the people, at a time when the covenant had all but disappeared. Elijah rejected any "watering down" of his religion. Only Yahweh was Lord in Israel and Elijah would not permit any idol to interfere in Yahweh's territory. In the contest on Mount Carmel, the prophet was not afraid to challenge everyone: "How long do you mean to hobble first on the one leg and then on the other? If Yahweh is God, follow Him; If Baal, follow him." (2 Kings 18:21).[6] It was not possible to serve both. Elijah, at the sacrifice on Mount Carmel, recalled his people to the faith of their ancestors.

At the same time, the prophet Elijah was not afraid to be creative in religious matters. When the people settled down in Israel, they began to forget God. Yahweh was very important to the Israelites when they were wandering in the desert, but seemed to have little to say in the new style of life in the Promised Land. The Israelites preferred to adore Baal, who was considered more useful to farmers inasmuch as he was the lord of the rain, the sunshine and of fertility in general, according to what was claimed by his followers. The image of Yahweh needed some modernisation. If Yahweh really was the true God of Israel, he had to be so in all the situations in which Israel might find itself. Elijah succeeded in transforming the image of Yahweh, showing that it was Yahweh and not Baal who sent the rain and fire from heaven. Yahweh was the Lord of Israel and not Baal. Elijah knew how to make the Word of God speak to his own times.

For the Jews, Elijah is still a living figure. For Christians, he represents a challenge to do in our times what he did in his. Despite the elements of our modern world that tend to distract us we must remain strong in the truth that we have received, but at the same time be able to translate this eternal truth for times that change continually. Faithfulness without creativity renders faith an anachronism; creativity without faithfulness abandons the faith for every passing fancy.

The function of Elijah in the post-biblical Jewish faith was that of being the precursor of the Messiah. This belief, which was common at the time of Jesus, is evidence that for the Jews Elijah was not – and is still not today – merely an historical figure, but is a living person. After Moses, Abraham and David, Elijah is the Old Testament figure most mentioned in the New Testament.

Using the Elijah saga cycle for prayer

The choice of the following texts from the Elijah saga cycle has been motivated by their usefulness for prayer. Obviously it is a personal choice. This book can

---

6   One can use any version of the Bible for prayer but the one I have chosen is the *New Jerusalem Bible*, (ed.) Henry Wansbrough, (New York & London: Doubleday / Darton, Longman & Todd, 1985). In this version the name "Yahweh" is used for the God of Israel. The Jewish people held and hold this name in such reverence that they do not normally pronounce it, using instead the term "Lord". Many versions of the Bible follow this custom.

be used by individuals or groups, and one can begin from whatever chapter seems most interesting. Before starting on the individual texts, I would like to say a word about the ancient method of prayer called *Lectio Divina* (holy reading). This method is the one used to help us in our reading the stories of the Prophet Elijah.

The texts of Sacred Scripture used in this book are taken from *The New Jerusalem Bible* but any translation can equally well be used. The words might be slightly different according to the translation but the sense will be the same.

The writing of the Word of God.
Window by George Walsh in the Chapel of Avila Discalced Carmelite Friary, Dublin.

What is *Lectio Divina*?

When we pray, in some way we enter into a relationship with God. Prayer is our response to God who first approaches us. The *Catechism of the Catholic Church* understands prayer firstly as a relationship with God and only secondly as a special activity. Article 2558 says:

> "Great is the mystery of the faith!" The Church professes this mystery in the Apostles' Creed (*Part One*) and celebrates it in the sacramental liturgy (*Part Two*), so that the life of the faithful may be conformed to Christ in the Holy Spirit to the glory of God the Father (*Part Three*). This mystery, then, requires that the faithful believe in it, that they celebrate it, and that they live from it in a vital and personal relationship with the living and true God. This relationship is prayer.

Personal relationships take time, energy and a commitment in order to develop. We must find something in common with the other person. What we have in common with God is Jesus Christ. He is the culmination of all that God has done for the world, and in Christ can be found everything that God wants to say to humanity. In the Scriptures we read the story of how God spoke to the people and what God wants to say. The whole of Scripture leads us to the fullness of the revelation of God in Christ Jesus. We cannot say that we want to know God if we ignore the divine message in Sacred Scripture. There is always something new to discover in the Scriptures.

The rediscovery of the centrality of the Word of God in the Church led to the rediscovery also of the ancient practice of *Lectio Divina* (holy reading). This was the normal way of prayer of the ancient monks and from them passed on to all the older religious orders. This way of prayer has had a profound effect on the history of Christian spirituality and can be said to be a constant in the Christian life. *Lectio Divina* is not only a method of prayer, but is a way of life; it is not simply yet another thing to be fitted in to our already overcrowded schedules, but rather is the element that shapes our whole day according to the will of God. It is, in fact, the form of all Christian prayer.

According to an ancient tradition, there are four fundamental moments in this way of prayer: Reading, Meditation, Prayer and Contemplation. Or to put these another way: Read, Reflect, Respond and Rest. These moments are not strictly separated but flow into each other naturally and other moments can be added.

Prayer is a very personal thing and each person must follow where the Spirit leads. The four traditional moments of *Lectio Divina* are simply an indication of the basic elements that make up Christian prayer.

Prayer is rather like soup. Good soup (prayer) has these four elements as basic ingredients, but each cook will have a different recipe. The soup will have a different taste according to the quantity of each ingredient and according to what other ingredients are added. We have a great freedom in our relationship with God but *Lectio Divina* contains the wisdom of centuries of living the Christian life. *Lectio Divina* is not a rigid method but changes according to the person who follows its rhythm.

Read

The first ingredient is *Lectio* (the traditional name), or, in other words, a time to read the Word of God. We can read the Scriptures in many ways. With the rosary "we read" the Word of God in the sense that the prayers come from the Sacred Scriptures. Looking at frescoes and stained glass windows was the way in which uneducated people in the Middle Ages could "read" the Scriptures. Of course these things can still speak very powerfully to us today. The same can be said for statues, tapestries and any way of telling the biblical stories. We can read the Sacred Scriptures during daily Mass and in the Prayer of the Church, the Office. To read the Word of God with profit, we must listen attentively in order to receive what God wants to give us. Clearly it is not sufficient to listen to the Word; we must also put it into practice, as Mary the mother of Jesus did (cf. *Luke* 11:27-28). It is possible to listen to the Scriptures in a perfunctory fashion without allowing the words to touch us. It is necessary to make an effort to receive what God wants to say to us at each moment.

The Word of God is the story of God's relationship with the human family; it is the story of my and your relationship with God. We learn from the Old and New Testaments how God speaks to us and what are the problems inherent in this dialogue. By means of the Word, God speaks personally to you and to me. God wants to say something particular to us, and if we do not listen we will not receive this very important message. When we read the Scriptures, it is necessary to take time, lest the Word goes in one ear and out the other without touching our hearts. It is important to reserve every day a little time to read or listen to the Word of God.

If one stops praying, it is difficult to get back into a rhythm. Although it is not necessary to be rigid in the exact time set aside, it is a commitment that must not be forgotten if we want to maintain a healthy relationship with God. There will also be days when all our plans are thrown into confusion and we hardly have time to bless ourselves. On those occasions we can say something like, "Today, Lord, I am really busy. Perhaps I will forget you. Please do not forget me!" However, these occasions must be an exception to the normal rhythm of our personal relationship with God.

Reflect

The second moment or ingredient of *Lectio Divina* is *meditatio*. This term, which means meditation, is very wide and so it is necessary to define it a little. In our western European tradition, to meditate is equivalent to reflect on God or on the things of God. In Buddhism, on the contrary it means "not thinking", and includes the various techniques used to arrive at this. Because of the influence of eastern religious practices, the normally accepted meaning of meditation in the world at large is this, and in particular because of the widespread use of "transcendental meditation". However there also remains the traditional idea of reflecting on God or on some point of our faith. In this type of meditation we try to enter more profoundly into the mystery of God or the mysteries of the faith. For example, we can spend a little time thinking about the Eucharist, starting from a text of Scripture. Then we could think about what the Eucharist means for us today. We receive Christ as our food so that we might begin to live like him. This is only one example among many of a meditation. We have a brain and we must use it also in the area of our faith life.

There is another type of meditation, more ancient than that described above. At the beginnings of Christianity, meditation involved the whole body. When the first Carmelite hermits lived on Mount Carmel in the early 13th century they understood meditation as a method for affixing the words of Sacred Scripture – and especially the psalms – in the mind and heart. Every hermit repeated the scriptural words over and over, with special emphasis on the psalms, in a loud voice. That is probably one reason their cells were originally quite far apart so that each would not be disturbed by the noise of the other. Gradually it was hoped that the Word of God would transform their hearts.

Meditation, then, can have for us today also these different meanings: to reflect on the Word of God in order to apply it to one's own life, or repeat the words slowly in order to fix them in the heart. What does this Word say to me today, or what does the Lord want to say to me at this particular moment?

It can be useful to consult a Bible commentary. In the following chapters you will find a brief comment on the chosen text. It is only to help the reader to enter more easily into the Word of God presented by these ancient stories. It is not necessary to spend much time studying the text, but it is important to take a moment in order to get an idea of what God really is saying and so avoid the risk of making the Word say what we want to hear.

Respond

The third traditional moment or ingredient of *Lectio Divina* is *oratio*, which means prayer. This is our response to the Word of God. You may wonder has not everything we have been doing up to this point not also been prayer? Of course. However, according to the ancient monks from whom we have received *Lectio Divina*, prayer was understood as an opportunity for a heart-to-heart dialogue with God. The two previous moments – reading the Word and reflecting on it – are really a preparation for this intimate conversation with God. This intimate dialogue can take place in the midst of our normal daily tasks and can easily interchange with moments of meditation. For example, while we are working we could perhaps think about the passage of Scripture that we had chosen, or, like the monks of antiquity, we might choose to repeat some word or phrase so that the Word of God might take hold of our heart. We have to adapt ourselves to the circumstances of our lives. These words or our thoughts are aimed at touching our heart and starting a real dialogue with God. The conversation with the Lord can take many forms and is very personal. If it starts to rain and you are caught without an umbrella, your prayer might be one of complaint. If you are very worried, your prayer will probably focus on what you are worried about. You can praise or thank God. The psalms cover the whole spectrum of human emotion and they teach us that we can speak with God about anything. The goal of *Lectio Divina* is to open the human heart to God so that it might be transformed.

Spontaneous prayer sooner or later tends to diminish and silence becomes more and more normal. In the silence we leave a space for the Spirit of God to pray in us. Scripture says: "The Spirit too comes to help us in our weakness, for, when we do not know how to pray properly, then the Spirit personally makes our petitions for us in groans that cannot be put into words; and he who can see into all hearts knows what the Spirit means because the prayers that the Spirit makes for God's holy people are always in accordance with the mind of God." (*Romans* 8:26-27).

Rest

The traditional name for the fourth moment or ingredient of *Lectio Divina* is *contemplatio* or contemplation. This is a concept with a lot of history behind it and not a few difficulties connected to it. I prefer to use a more common term that is easily understandable: rest. At this point we are invited to enter into the mystery of God. It is no longer necessary to think holy thoughts, or to speak but simply to rest in God. "Come to me, all you who labour and are overburdened, and I will give you rest. Shoulder my yoke and learn from me, for I am gentle and humble in heart, and you will find rest for your souls. Yes, my yoke is easy and my burden light." (*Matthew* 11:28-30).

When our prayer becomes silence, perhaps it may seem that we are wasting time. There will be a temptation to return to a form of prayer where we were in control, or at least where we had the sensation of doing something. However, silence is a normal development of prayer. There comes a time when we must leave behind our beautiful words because they cannot express what is in our heart. In silence, God can listen to what is in our heart and we can listen to the still small voice of God.

According to the *Catechism of the Catholic Church*:

> **2712** Contemplative prayer is the prayer of the child of God, of the forgiven sinner who agrees to welcome the love by which he is loved and who wants to respond to it by loving even more. But he knows that the love he is returning is poured out by the Spirit in his heart, for everything is grace from God. Contemplative prayer is the poor and humble surrender to the loving will of the Father in ever deeper union with his beloved Son.

> **2713** Contemplative prayer is the simplest expression of the mystery of prayer. It is a gift, a grace; it can be accepted only in humility and poverty. Contemplative prayer is a covenant relationship established by God within our hearts. Contemplative prayer is a *communion* in which the Holy Trinity conforms man, the image of God, "to his likeness."

> **2714** Contemplative prayer is also the pre-eminently intense time of prayer. In it the Father strengthens our inner being with power through his Spirit "that Christ may dwell in [our] hearts through faith" and we may be "grounded in love."

2715 Contemplation is a *gaze* of faith, fixed on Jesus. "I look at him and he looks at me": this is what a certain peasant of Ars used to say to his holy curé about his prayer before the tabernacle. This focus on Jesus is a renunciation of self. His gaze purifies our heart; the light of the countenance of Jesus illumines the eyes of our heart and teaches us to see everything in the light of his truth and his compassion for all men. Contemplation also turns its gaze on the mysteries of the life of Christ. Thus it learns the "interior knowledge of our Lord," the more to love him and follow him.

2716 Contemplative prayer is *hearing* the Word of God. Far from being passive, such attentiveness is the obedience of faith, the unconditional acceptance of a servant, and the loving commitment of a child. It participates in the "Yes" of the Son become servant and the Fiat of God's lowly handmaid.

2717 Contemplative prayer is *silence*, the "symbol of the world to come" or "silent love." Words in this kind of prayer are not speeches; they are like kindling that feeds the fire of love. In this silence, unbearable to the "outer" man, the Father speaks to us his incarnate Word, who suffered, died, and rose; in this silence the Spirit of adoption enables us to share in the prayer of Jesus.

2718 Contemplative prayer is a union with the prayer of Christ insofar as it makes us participate in his mystery. The mystery of Christ is celebrated by the Church in the Eucharist, and the Holy Spirit makes it come alive in contemplative prayer so that our charity will manifest it in our acts.

2719 Contemplative prayer is a communion of love bearing Life for the multitude, to the extent that it consents to abide in the night of faith. The Paschal night of the Resurrection passes through the night of the agony and the tomb – the three intense moments of the Hour of Jesus which his Spirit (and not "the flesh [which] is weak") brings to life in prayer. We must be willing to "keep watch with [him] one hour."

When we read the Word of God, or meditate on it or pray about it, we are using our own words and thoughts, but the Word belongs to God and possibly God wants to comment on it. God often does this by inspiring a thought or a feeling. The ancient monks believed that it was important to leave some time for God, and they called this time *contemplation* (contemplation). Many people can be rather suspicious of this word. By calling cloistered nuns "contemplatives" we may often think that we can leave contemplation to them. However if we translate the word "contemplation" by another term like, "an intimate relationship with God in Jesus Christ", we can perhaps begin to see that it cannot be exclusive to cloistered nuns. Contemplation is for everyone.

The fruit of prayer is not the brilliant ideas that we may have about Scripture or the feelings of love that rise up in our heart. At times it is impossible to have a single holy thought. The fruit of prayer can only be seen outside the time of prayer in the way we relate with others on a regular basis. If our prayer is authentic, our life will begin to change, probably not in extraordinary ways, but in the small details of daily life. It is quite possible that we ourselves may not be at all aware of any of these changes, but they will begin to strike those with whom we live and work.

We need some quiet time when we leave behind our own words, thoughts, and ideas and simply rest in God, who loves us with a love that goes beyond anything we would imagine. In the first Appendix I suggest a method of silent prayer. This method is based above all on the work of Fr. Thomas Keating, O.C.S.O.[7] It is a method that helps one move from the third phase of *Lectio Divina*, that of responding to God in spontaneous prayer (*oratio*) in order to simply wait for God in silence, so that we will be ready when and if God wishes to bring us into greater depths. This method can be a preparation for contemplative prayer (*contemplatio*).

Act

Finally in this book I add a fifth moment or ingredient of *Lectio Divina*: *actio* (action), which is also important because it moves prayer into daily life. The goal of Christian prayer is to enter into an intimate relationship with God but this process must have effects in daily life. According to the *First letter of John*:

> My dear friends, let us love one another, since love is from God and everyone who loves is a child of God and knows God. Whoever fails to love does not know God, because God is love. This is the revelation of God's love for us, that God sent his only Son into the world that we might have life through him. Love consists in this: it is not we who loved God, but God loved us and sent his Son to

---

7   *Open Mind, Open Heart*, (Massachusetts: Element Books, 1992). For a simple introduction to this method of prayer and its background, see Elizabeth Smith and Joseph Chalmers, *A Deeper Love*, (Tunbridge Wells, Kent: Burns & Oates, and New York: Continuum, 1999).

expiate our sins. My dear friends, if God loved us so much, we too should love one another. No one has ever seen God, but as long as we love one another God remains in us and his love comes to its perfection in us. (*I John* 4:7-12).

The example of the prophet Elijah can help us to remain faithful to God in times that are not always easy. Let us journey together with Elijah.

The prophet Elijah (Elias) being fed by ravens.
Window at St. Edward the Confessor Church, Dringhouses, York.

Reflection 1
<u>THE PROPHET ELIJAH</u>
1 Kings **17:1-6**

<u>Invocation</u>

We ask for the presence of the Holy Spirit so that our prayer will be according to God's will.

Father, send your Holy Spirit to bring light to my heart so that your Word may become the centre of my existence. The prophet Elijah appeared without any introduction to accomplish your will in a complicated situation. Give me the wisdom to know your will and the courage to put it into practice in all the situations of my life. I make this humble prayer to You, Father, through Jesus Christ your beloved Son, by the power of the Holy Spirit. Amen.

<u>Text</u>

Read attentively the following text for the first time in order to get an idea of the overall sense and to take in the details of the story from *1 Kings* 17.

> [1] Elijah the Tishbite, of Tishbe in Gilead, said to Ahab, 'By the life of Yahweh, God of Israel, whom I serve, there will be neither dew nor rain these coming years unless I give the word.' [2] The word of Yahweh came to him, [3] 'Go away from here, go east and hide by the torrent of Cherith, east of the Jordan. [4] You can drink from the stream, and I have ordered the ravens to bring you food there.' [5] So he set out and did as Yahweh had said; he went and stayed by the torrent of Cherith, east of the Jordan. [6] The ravens brought him bread in the morning and meat in the evening, and he quenched his thirst at the stream.

<u>Read</u>

What does this text mean? In order to understand what it is about, it is important also to read some preceding verses, which sum up the rule of King Ahab. This will go some way to explain the reason for the words and actions of the prophet Elijah.

See *1 Kings* 16:29-34 on the reign of Ahab (874-853 B.C.)

> [29] Ahab son of Omri became king of Israel in the thirty-eighth year of Asa king of Judah, and reigned over Israel for twenty-two years in Samaria. [30] Ahab son of Omri did what is displeasing to Yahweh, and was worse than all his predecessors. [31] The least that he did was to follow the sinful example of Jeroboam son of Nebat: he married Jezebel daughter of Ethbaal, king of the Sidonians, and then proceeded to serve Baal and worship him. [32] He erected an altar to him in the temple of Baal which he built in Samaria. [33] Ahab also put up a sacred pole and committed other crimes as well, provoking the anger of Yahweh, God of Israel, more than all the kings of Israel his predecessors. [34] It was in his time that Hiel of Bethel rebuilt Jericho. Laying its foundations cost him his eldest son Abiram and erecting its gates cost him his youngest son Segub, just as Yahweh had foretold through Joshua son of Nun.

The *First Book of the Kings* is part of a bigger history; the interest of this history is to explain why the monarchy failed in Israel. According to the particular view of the author of the sacred texts, the kings of Israel basically were not faithful to God. The monarchy tried to transform the Lord, Yahweh, into a national god at the service of the kingdom and its interests. Clearly, according to the writer, King Ahab, like his father, was an enemy of God and of the true religion.

The biography of Elijah, which was one of the sources that the author used, must have begun by introducing the prophet. The author of the *Books of the Kings* omits this introductory part because his interest is to awaken faith and not to respond to human curiosity. We are presented with the prophet suddenly, in the act of announcing a long drought to King Ahab. Elijah appeared on the scene at a critical moment in the struggle against religious syncretism. Ahab, the king of Israel, married Jezebel, the princess of Tyre. Her religion was Baalism, which was based on the idea that in some way human beings must relate to and placate the mysterious forces that surround them. They did this by means of ritual and these powers were often personified and presented as gods (Baal). King Ahab allowed Jezebel and her servants to continue the practice of their own religion in Israel. A temple dedicated to Baal was built in Samaria (*1 Kings* 16:32). This was nothing more than Solomon had done for his foreign wives. (*1 Kings* 11:1-8). However Jezebel was rather different from Solomon's wives. She maintained 450 prophets of Baal and 400 prophets of the female idol Asherah (*1 Kings* 18:19). There were many more prophets than the queen would have needed for her own private devotions and there can be no doubt that the work of these prophets was the active propagation of their faith among the Israelites. Jezebel was fixed in her idea of substituting Baal for Yahweh and getting rid of the traditional religion of Israel.

At a certain point, Queen Jezebel began to persecute the followers of Yahweh and had success in the sense that the opposition was forced to go underground. But a profound hatred was being stored up in the hearts of the Israelites. It was the prophet Elijah who crystallised the opposition to Jezebel.

Elijah then appeared on the scene without any prior presentation to proclaim the judgement of God in this situation of apostasy. Elijah announced the beginning of a great drought to King Ahab as a divine punishment for his obstinate attachment to the cult of Baal. Perhaps it was not a punishment but a sign from God that it was He, and not Baal who gave the rain, which was so necessary for the crops and indeed for life itself. Baal was the God of fertility and of the rain according to his followers. Elijah, with the announcement of the drought, proclaimed that Yahweh was God in Israel and only Yahweh could grant rain and the growth of crops. This was tantamount to a declaration of war!

The name of Elijah, which means, "Yahweh is my God", tells us a great deal about him. According to the book of *Exodus* (20:3), God will not have other gods before Him. Elijah is faithful to the ancient covenant with Yahweh, the God of Israel. The concept of covenant that God made with certain individuals (Noah, Abraham etc) and with the whole chosen people is fundamental to the Bible. A covenant was a bond that united God and the people. The phrase that occurs often throughout the Bible to describe the nature of the covenant is: *I shall be your God and you shall be my people* (e.g. *Exodus* 6:7). Elijah is the servant of Yahweh, the God who has made a covenant with the people of Israel. God is always faithful and demands faithfulness from the people.

In the mentality of the times, drought was interpreted as a punishment from God for the sin of unfaithfulness. After the description of the reign of Ahab with all his sins, Elijah appears to announce the drought as the punishment of God. After this announcement, Elijah receives God's command to go east where he will have enough to eat and drink. It seems that the prophet's life is in danger. God has ordered the ravens to bring food to Elijah. According to the Bible, ravens are impure creatures (*Leviticus* 11:15; *Deuteronomy* 14:14), and certainly good Israelites would not have touched them. Some biblical scholars suggest that the word "ravens" might be translated also as "Arabs". In Hebrew there is not much difference in how one writes "Arabs" and "ravens". Certainly receiving food from ravens is miraculous but is it any less miraculous if instead of ravens it were Arabs who had fed the prophet of Israel?

Reflect

Read again the text of *1 Kings* 17:1-6, printed above.

What does God want to say to me (to us) at this moment by means of this Bible text? To help our reflection and the application of the Word of God to daily life, I will propose some questions. This is not a test. There is neither one particular correct answer nor a wrong one. Your answers might help you to deepen your relationship with God. Take whatever time you need for each question:

1. How do you feel, faced by the power of God, as shown by the prophet Elijah when he announces the drought?

2. The Word of God came to Elijah. How does God speak to you?

3. Elijah is the servant of Yahweh the Lord. How do you serve God?

4. The Prophet Elijah followed the commandment of God to leave and hide near the brook called Cherith (or Kerith). What decisions have you taken to change direction in your life according to what you believed was the will of God?

5. God ordered the ravens (Arabs?) to give food to the prophet. How and when have you experienced the Providence of God?

6. How do you feel, faced with these questions?

Respond

What does your heart want to say to God now? What do you feel? Are you angry with God? Do you not want to change your life? Perhaps you are quite content with your prejudices or perhaps you are thankful for all that God has done for you? There is no feeling that is unacceptable. Prayer is a relationship with God and every relationship is different. We see in the psalms a great variety of human emotions in relation to God. We can find various prayers in Sacred Scripture or in Christian Tradition. Perhaps some of the words below respond to what you feel.

We praise you, O God:
we acclaim you as the Lord.
Everlasting Father,
all the world bows down before you.

All the angels sing your praise,
the hosts of heaven and all the angelic powers.
All the cherubim and seraphim
call out to you in unending song:

Holy, Holy, Holy
is the Lord God of angel hosts.

The heavens and the earth are filled
with your majesty and glory.[8]

It is important to give yourself some space so that your heart has the opportunity to speak directly to God with your own words, even if these do not seem to be as beautiful as those of Sacred Scripture or of the Church.

Rest

There is a profound hunger in the human heart. Nothing is ever enough; we always seek something more. Only God can satisfy the infinite hunger of the human heart. The tragedy of human existence is that we often seek to placate this growing need with what is not God. All these things satisfy only in part and for a short period of time but not forever.

The prophet Elijah is the spiritual father of the Carmelite Order in the sense that the Order sees in the prophet an inspiration for faithfully living according to the will of God. The whole of Carmelite spirituality is directed towards transformation. To be transformed means to attain what we were created to be, inasmuch as this is possible on this earth. Christ is the prototype of a new humanity; our task is to become like him and to incarnate some aspect of the divine in human nature. In this way we co-operate in the transformation of our world. However, we can do nothing without him: it is he who brings about our transformation, but will not do so without our collaboration. Transformation is a mystery in that it has to do with what happens in the heart of the human being who co-operates with God to become a new man or a new woman, God's

---

8   From the *Te Deum*, a traditional prayer of the Church.

masterpiece. What happens in the heart must, of course, have effects in how the individual lives his or her daily life.

The ultimate goal of *Lectio Divina* is to have so matured in friendship with Jesus Christ to the point where his values become our values and we begin to see with the eyes of God and to love with the heart of God. An authentic friendship with God must be expressed in a commitment to serve others in some way.

There is something tragic in the human condition. The biblical writers call it, *The Fall* and attribute all the problems of the world to human sin. Whatever the reason, there is without doubt something wrong, something that ruins even the best of intentions. We are born with natural instincts, which, over the course of years, tend to become voracious needs. For example, we are born with a need to be loved, to have some control over our lives, and simply to survive, both on a physical and psychological level. Very easily these basic human needs end up by coming into conflict with other people and their needs. There is a profound egoism in every human being that, if left uncontrolled, will imprison us. These instincts, together with the conditioning that we receive as we grow up from our culture and social surroundings, go to form the *false self*.[9] There are various ways of describing and explaining the false self. I want to say very simply that it is by means of the false self that we seek to save ourselves instead of trusting ourselves to God who alone can save us.

The false self leads to misery and to death and so transformation is essential. The spiritual journey leads to transformation, which is the death of the false self and the coming to birth of the true self, made in the image and likeness of God. It is truly a question of life and death because the one who seeks to save his life will lose it, but the one who loses his life for the sake of the Gospel will save it (*Matthew* 10:39; *Mark* 8:35; *Luke* 9:24).

We begin the journey of our transformation when we respond to God who calls us to seriously consider our relationship with Him. We can also let a number of years go by, years of preparation for this journey of the spirit in which we must try and try again to reach an understanding of our real spiritual needs. Perhaps we will have received various "wake-up calls" in the course of our life, various warnings from God, events that have shaken us up, that have indicated to us what God wants from us.

What happens when we decide to take God seriously? Saint Teresa of Jesus (of Avila), in a famous example, describes the human being as a castle, which

---

9   See Thomas Keating, *Invitation to Love*, (Element, Massachusetts & Dorset, 1992), chapters 1-4, and Elizabeth Smith & Joseph Chalmers, *A Deeper Love*, chapter 8.

is made up of many rooms.[10] The door of the castle is prayer and it seems that many people do not even get beyond the door. The first rooms of the castle are called the rooms of self-knowledge,[11] which must accompany every step of the spiritual journey. According to Saint Teresa, humility means to "walk in the truth",[12] to know and accept the truth about ourselves. Self-knowledge is not easy and often we prefer to remain in a situation of profound self-delusion. Our vocation is to be transformed by God in order to become like God, learning to see with God's eyes and love with a divinised heart. I have been called to walk this road of transformation as a Carmelite priest. Each person has his or her own road to travel and life to live. God knows us profoundly, and the state to which we are called (married, single, priest, religious) is for us the road we must travel to arrive at our transformation.

The false self, which surrounds us like a cocoon, must be destroyed so that we can experience the freedom of the children of God. The first step consists in recognising and accepting what we really are. If we do not do this, we will continue to live in a world of illusion. The false self is an expert at disguise. Life in family, or in community, reveals who you are because you cannot hide when you have to live with other people. During the courtship period perhaps one can present one's best side, but after the wedding, the other side begins to assert itself. It is much better when husband and wife commit themselves to the spiritual journey together because, in this case, each will be able to understand the difficulties that the other has to face. It is to be hoped that in a religious community all the members are committed to walking the spiritual path.

We can surround ourselves with all sorts of excuses for the way we live or for what we do in particular situations. These become so habitual and we tend to get used to little refusals of what God is asking of us that we no longer notice the contradiction. The false self easily persuades us that we are in the right and that some proposals of the Gospel do not apply to us. God is always present, but we have the power to block the action of the Spirit, and the false self wants precisely this because it grasps intuitively that following the Spirit will be its destruction. God transforms us by means of everyday life and not just when we are engaged in what we consider to be holy pursuits. We have to co-operate in daily life. It is not sufficient just to say some prayers or even a lot of prayers. We must seek to put God's will into action in the smallest details of our lives.

10 *Interior Castle* in the *Complete Works of St. Teresa of Avila.* There are two important English translations. The earlier is that of E. Allison Peers, *Complete Works of St. Teresa,* (London: Sheed & Ward, 1957). The later is by Kieran Kavanaugh & Otilio Rodriguez, *The Collected Works of St. Teresa of Avila,* (Washington D.C.: ICS Publications, 1976).
11 *Interior Castle*, I, 1-2.
12 *Interior Castle*, VI, 10,7.

We begin very gradually to reorganise our lives according to the message of Jesus Christ. We leave behind grave sin and this often is no easy matter, but the suffering involved in doing so is soon submerged by the initial joy of following Christ. As we become used to living a Christian life, there is the danger of falling into habit. If we really intend to follow the will of God and to put it into practice, we will meet obstacles and the false self will rebel against every attempt to attack it. This interior conflict causes difficulties and obscurity. This obscurity can be a time of suffering, but if we remain faithful God will heal the wounds caused by the false self and will set us free to become all that God created us to be.

What are these obstacles? The false self system is based on the lie that we can reach perfect happiness if we receive sufficient esteem, if we have control over our life and feel secure. Given that we have been created with an infinite capacity, we seek infinite quantities of affection, security and control. When we try to shift our focus from worldly things to religious matters, also the false self begins to move in the same direction and feels perfectly at home in a religious situation. However, the false self is always centred on itself no matter where it happens to find itself.

We must always remember that God loves us and does everything for our growth and transformation. When we encounter difficulties on the way, it is a great help to try to see the hand of God at work. What is God saying within the particular situations in which we find ourselves? Can we learn something about ourselves from our responses to the problems of life?

We need periods of silence when we let go of all our preoccupations and listen to the voice of God who often speaks without words. We must be very silent in order to discern what God is saying to us. Now I suggest that you take a moment for prayer. You will find some simple guidelines for the "prayer of silence" in Appendix I towards the end of this book. Another term for this form of prayer is the "prayer in secret" in the sense of the Gospel according to Matthew: "But when you pray, go to your private room, shut yourself in, and so pray to your Father who is in that secret place, and your Father who sees all that is done in secret will reward you." (*Matthew* 6:6).

Act

Prayer is not an isolated practice; it must have some effect in one's life. The fruit of prayer can be discerned in the midst of daily life, in how we habitually treat those with whom we live, with whom we work or those we meet on a casual basis. Saint Paul describes the fruit of the Holy Spirit in one's life. If our prayer is authentic, this fruit will grow within us:

> On the other hand the fruit of the Spirit is love, joy, peace, patience, kindness, goodness, trustfulness, gentleness and self-control; no law can touch such things as these. (*Galatians* 5:22-23)

From your reading of the Word of God or from your own prayer, perhaps some word or phrase has struck you that can accompany you during the day to remind you of the presence of God. Prayer must be incarnated in the reality of every day. Inside us we have the equivalent of a tape or compact disc (or mini-disc or MP3 player for those who are more up to date!). These tapes or discs contain the memory of everything we have lived through as well as our reactions to these events. I have already said that the process of contemplation transforms the human heart and gives us another perspective, which is the perspective of God. Before we think of seeing from God's point of view, it would be interesting to try to see the world from the perspective of another person. This is really impossible, but the attempt helps us to emerge from our solitude and our selfishness, and at least begin to understand why someone acts in a particular way. These internal tapes make comments in all the situations in which we find ourselves. Naturally these comments are normally in our own favour and against others.

One can use a phrase or a word from Sacred Scripture to rewrite the internal disc along with a positive commentary instead of the habitual one. During the day, let this phrase or word reverberate within you, especially in moments of difficulty or when you are tempted to respond to someone else with anger or irony.

Perhaps a word or a phrase comes spontaneously to mind from your own prayer. If not, you might decide to choose some word to use during the day taking it from the Scripture text we have been using for prayer. For example:

"the God of Israel, whom I serve"

"the Word of Yahweh came to him"

"go away from here"

"he did as Yahweh had said"

The important thing is to remember the presence of God throughout the whole day, in the highs and lows of ordinary life. Allow your relationship with the Lord to permeate your whole life.

The prophet Elijah responded with faith to the command of God. Faith is not always easy. Faith helps us to see the world and to react to it like God. Saint Paul, in his *Letter to the Romans*, teaches what is implied in a life of faith:

> [9] Let love be without any pretence. Avoid what is evil; stick to what is good. [10] In brotherly love let your feelings of deep affection for one another come to expression and regard others as more important than yourself. [11] In the service of the Lord, work not half-heartedly but with conscientiousness and an eager spirit. [12] Be joyful in hope, persevere in hardship; keep praying regularly; [13] share with any of God's holy people who are in need; look for opportunities to be hospitable. [14] Bless your persecutors; never curse them, bless them. [15] Rejoice with others when they rejoice, and be sad with those in sorrow. [16] Give the same consideration to all others alike. Pay no regard to social standing, but meet humble people on their own terms. Do not congratulate yourself on your own wisdom. [17] Never pay back evil with evil, but bear in mind the ideals that all regard with respect. [18] As much as possible, and to the utmost of your ability, be at peace with everyone. (*Romans* 12: 9-18).

What do you need to do in order to live your faith in God today?

The prophet Elijah with the Widow of Zarephath and her Son.
Window in the Cathedral of Notre-Dame, Chartres, France.

Reflection 2
AT ZAREPHATH –
THE MIRACLE OF THE FLOUR AND THE OIL
1 Kings 17:7-16

Invocation

Let us pray that we will be filled with the presence of the Holy Spirit.

Father, in a time of drought and hunger, you provided for your prophet Elijah so that he could become an instrument of your will. Elijah experienced the generosity of the widow and brought out great faith with his request. Help me with the gift of your Holy Spirit to have the faith of Elijah and of the widow and a generosity towards You. I entrust my entire life to your presence and your purifying and transforming action within me. I make this prayer to You, Holy Father, in the name of Jesus Christ, your Son, through the power of your Spirit. Amen.

Text

Read attentively the following text for the first time to get the overall sense and the details of the story.

> [7] But after a while the stream dried up, for the country had had no rain. [8] And then the word of Yahweh came to Elijah, [9] 'Up and go to Zarephath in Sidonia, and stay there. I have ordered a widow there to give you food.' [10] So he went off to Sidon. And when he reached the city gate, there was a widow gathering sticks. Addressing her he said, 'Please bring a little water in a pitcher for me to drink.' [11] She was on her way to fetch it when he called after her. 'Please', he said, 'bring me a scrap of bread in your hand.' [12] 'As Yahweh your God lives,' she replied, 'I have no baked bread, but only a handful of meal in a jar and a little oil in a jug; I am just gathering a stick or two to go and prepare this for myself and my son to eat, and then we shall die.' [13] But Elijah said to her, 'Do not be afraid, go and do as you have said; but first make a little scone of it for me and bring

it to me, and then make some for yourself and for your son. [14] For Yahweh, God of Israel, says this: Jar of meal shall not be spent, jug of oil shall not be emptied, before the day when Yahweh sends rain on the face of the earth.' [15] The woman went and did as Elijah told her and they ate the food, she, himself and her son. [16] The jar of meal was not spent nor the jug of oil emptied, just as Yahweh had foretold through Elijah.

Read

The drought continues and the water at Kerith eventually dries up. Elijah receives the order from God (v.7-9) to go to Zarephath (sometimes called Zarepta or Sareptha). This is followed by two miracles: the multiplication of the flour and oil (v.7-16), and the resurrection of the woman's son (v.17-24). As a response to the generosity of the widow of Zarephath, her food does not run out. This is another indication that it is Yahweh and not Baal who is Lord of the elements. The rain, stopped by Yahweh, has caused the famine, but God gives food to his faithful also outside the bounds of Israel. Zarephath was a city in Sidonia, the territory of Baal, but it is Yahweh who causes the drought and who protects his own, and it does not matter where they are to be found.

God works through a poor widow with very few resources to display the divine power. By means of this woman, God provides food for the prophet and also for the widow and her son. God chose a woman from Sidonia, who was completely different from another woman of the same race: Jezebel.

The miraculous multiplication of the flour and the oil is the reward for the self-effacing love of the poor widow. Jesus uses this story (*Luke* 4:25-26) in his inaugural sermon in order to point out the incomprehension of Israel towards the prophets.

> There were many widows in Israel, I can assure you, in Elijah's day, when heaven remained shut for three years and six months, and a great famine raged throughout the land; but Elijah was not sent to any one of these: he was sent to a widow at Zarephath, a town in Sidonia.

The woman of Sidonia became a prototype for other women outside Israel who received the grace of God through their meeting with Jesus (*Matthew* 15:21-28; *Mark* 7:24-30). The Canaanite woman of the Gospels is presented by Jesus as a model of faith. By means of the woman's continual request, Jesus seems to have changed his mind about his own mission. He understood that his mission must embrace all people. For the Fathers of the Church this widow is an exemplar of all the pagans who are called to the faith.

Reflect

Read again slowly the text of *1 Kings* 17:7-16.

Some questions to assist our reflection:

1. The water dried up in the brook. Are there any situations that have forced you to change direction in life?

2. How do you feel now, looking back at these situations?

3. God provided food for Elijah by means of the generosity of the widow. When and where have you experienced the generosity and the providence of God?

4. Who has been generous with you?

5. Are you generous? Really?

6. How do you feel when faced with the faith of Elijah and the widow?

7. Elijah said to the widow, "Do not be afraid". What do you fear and what helps you to trust in God?

Respond

Having read the text and reflected on it, what arises in your heart? Do you want to discuss with God the unjust treatment of the widow? Do you want to pray for a greater faith or generosity? Give yourself some space so that your heart has the opportunity to open up to God.

In the Bible, faith is the centre and the source of all religion. We can use the prayers of biblical figures to help us. Here is an example of a psalm. According to the tradition, it is a prayer of King David. We can use the feelings that are expressed in the psalm below (131:1-2) and apply them to our own situations:

> Yahweh, my heart is not haughty,
> I do not set my sights too high.
> I have taken no part in great affairs,
> in wonders beyond my scope.

> No, I hold myself in quiet and silence,
> like a little child in its mother's arms,
> like a little child, so I keep myself.

As well as reading this psalm it is important that your heart speak directly to God with your own words or without any words at all.

Rest

Contemplation is a gift of God but we can and we must prepare the soil of the heart for the divine visit. The preparation consists initially in living a good Christian life, following the message of the Gospel in daily life. It is useful to remember the words of Saint Paul in the *Letter to the Romans* (7:15):

> I do not understand my own behaviour; I do not act as I mean to,
> but I do things that I hate.

This is the common experience of the people who try to live the Gospel seriously. To really prepare ourselves to receive the gift of God, we must do what we can to change our motivation but we must accept that only God can heal the roots of our sins and only God can give us the possibility to live the Gospel in depth. Only God can finally transform the human heart according to the divine plan of salvation.

At the beginning of his ministry, Jesus appealed to the people to repent and believe the Good News (*Mark* 1:14-15). To be sorry for one's sins is a part of repentance but it is not the whole story. The word "repent" in the Gospel (*metanoeite*) means literally "to turn round in the road". It is rather like doing a U-turn in a car when we find that we are heading in the wrong direction. In order to really respond profoundly to what Jesus is asking of us, we must stop for a moment, otherwise the frenetic pace of modern life gives us no time to reflect. Once we have stopped, we need to take a look at our lives. It is necessary to be realistic. If we think that, apart from one or two little faults, we are basically in good spiritual fettle, we will not understand the need for a radical change. We will not understand the need to change direction.

The fundamental fact of our existence is that God lives in us. In Saint John's Gospel, Jesus says that he is the vine and we are the branches and that if we live in him and he in us, we will produce abundant fruit, because outside of him we can do nothing (*John* 15:5). The image from Saint Teresa of Avila of the human soul like a castle with many rooms has become a classic of Christian spirituality. At the centre of this castle, in the innermost room, "the very secret exchanges between God and the soul take place".[13] Saint Teresa tells us that many people live completely unaware of the fact that God lives at the centre of their being.[14] This centre is the true self that is often hidden by many layers of falsity. The invitation of Jesus to repentance involves first of all becoming aware that we are not what we could be.

Our human ways of thinking, loving and behaving are limited and imperfect because we are human. They are subject to distortion by the selfish part of us and are manifestations of what is often called the *false self*. It is this false self that we must deny, that must die, so that the true self can come to the fore. The false self is that part of us which seeks happiness in ways that can never satisfy us completely, because we have been created by God, and nothing else can satisfy the human spirit. Saint Teresa of Avila said that, "Only God suffices".[15] To begin to confront the false self and its destructive effects within us is to take to heart the message of Jesus to repent and believe the Gospel. We could think of repentance as meaning changing the direction in which we look for happiness, moving away from selfishness and moving towards God in whom alone can we find lasting happiness.

The false self system is based on a lie that tells us we will arrive at happiness only when we are in control of our lives, and when we receive the esteem and affection that we need. Given that we have been created with an infinite capacity, we will seek infinite amounts of affection, security and control. When we seek to change our focus from worldly to religious things, the false self follows us and does not change profoundly; only the exterior initially changes. We need a profound conversion before the heart will change.

What God wants to do in us is recreate us as the image of Christ. This is the true self that must emerge from the cocoon of the old self. From our earliest years, we learn how to respond to the world at large and to other people. We protect ourselves from perceived dangers and we always seek our own happiness. Gradually we construct emotional programmes to protect ourselves and which we believe will assure our happiness.[16] Within each of us there is an instinct for survival and this is a good thing. It stops us from walking in the middle of a busy highway and so on but it also pushes us to seek security in various subtle

---

13   *Interior Castle*, I, 1, 3.
14   *Interior Castle*, I, 1, 5.
15   The last line of what is commonly called *Saint Teresa's Bookmark*. It can be found among her poems in the Peers translation of her works.
16   For the concept of 'emotional programmes' see Thomas Keating, *Invitation to Love*, pp. 5-13. On the false self see Smith & Chalmers, *A Deeper Love*, chapter 8.

ways. However, we are called to the light of faith which means that we place our hope and trust in God alone. Only in God can we find lasting happiness. This is not easy, and our tendency is to believe in God while at the same time we put our trust in that which we think can give us security. We can say to God that we have faith in Him alone but the reality can often be different.

We need love and we seek this love in many different ways. However, this need or profound human desire can easily become distorted. We can take our self-image and our dignity from the level of love or affection that we receive. There is the temptation to manipulate people in order to gratify our own needs or wishes. However, we are good and worthy of love because God has created us and loves us. The divine presence manifests itself in each human being in a different way. Every woman and man reflects a tiny element of the beauty of God. In some people this is more difficult to perceive than in others! It does not matter what people think of us; the truth remains that we are good and lovable. Little by little we must recognise our desire for self-gratification in the area of our need for affection. Gradually we must let God change our hearts so that we are enabled to receive divine love. We are not – nor can we ever be – defined by the opinion of others.

One can also perceive the world as a threatening place and in order to feel secure we can try to control the situations in which we find ourselves. There is a tendency to seek to have power over things and over people in order to maintain our control and so feel secure.

These three so-called *emotional centres* – survival, esteem and control – exist in each one of us in some way or another. Perhaps we tend more strongly to one of these for a particular period in life or even permanently. These emotional centres affect us in very subtle ways. For example, with regard to the spiritual life, God must teach us that we cannot turn God on and off like a hot water tap. We do not believe for one minute that we are trying to control or manipulate God and so our attachment to our emotional programmes for happiness is so subtle. We often cling on to feelings or consolations during prayer because these give us a sense of making some progress on the spiritual journey. Often we will experience nothing during prayer so that we will learn by experience that only God, and no spiritual gift, no matter how exalted, can fully satisfy us.

It is important to have a rhythm of prayer because prayer is the sacred time that we dedicate to the Lord. It is good to think of God, to speak with God, using words from the Bible or our own words, but it is also important simply to be in silence before God because according to Saint John of the Cross "silent love is the language that God understands best".[17] To be in silence is not always easy. For this reason, I suggest the use of some method like the *prayer of silence* that can be found in the first Appendix.

Act

Choose a phrase from the Bible text above or from your own prayer to help you remember the presence of God in daily life, for example:

"the stream dried up"

"the Word of Yahweh came to him"

"up and go"

"do not be afraid"

"do as you have said"

"Yahweh, God of Israel says this"

Use the word or phrase that you have chosen during the day to fill your life with the Word of God. This word gradually writes over the internal tape or compact disc, which I mentioned in the previous reflection, that is the commentaries and prejudices that come spontaneously to mind. The goal is so that we can respond in every situation, not immediately from our own habitual selfish perspectives, but from the perspective of the new woman or man, recreated in Christ. This process of transformation is a long journey and our internal compact disc cannot be rewritten in a day. This spiritual journey takes at least a lifetime and we encounter many highs and lows. The transformation of the human heart is radical and profound; it is worthwhile continuing this journey despite all the difficulties that are encountered because our destiny is to become like God, or to use a term often employed by the ancient Fathers of the Church, "divinised".

The widow in the story showed great charity. Every day we have opportunities to live this essential Christian virtue. Try to be attentive today to everything that goes on around you. Is God perhaps asking you to show care to someone?

---

17 Maxims and Counsels, 53. As with St. Teresa, so also with John of the Cross, there are two major translations of the complete works. The older is E. Allison Peers, *The Complete Works of St. John of the Cross*, (London: Burns & Oates, 1954). The more recent is Kieran Kavanaugh and Otilio Rodriguez, *The Collected Works of St. John of the Cross*, (Washington D.C.: ICS Publications, 1979).

According to the *First Letter to the Corinthians* (chapter 13):

> [1] Though I command languages both human and angelic – if I speak without love, I am no more than a gong booming or a cymbal clashing. [2] And though I have the power of prophecy, to penetrate all mysteries and knowledge, and though I have all the faith necessary to move mountains – if I am without love, I am nothing. [3] Though I should give away to the poor all that I possess, and even give up my body to be burned – if I am without love, it will do me no good whatever. [4] Love is always patient and kind; love is never jealous; love is not boastful or conceited, [5] it is never rude and never seeks its own advantage, it does not take offence or store up grievances. [6] Love does not rejoice at wrongdoing, but finds its joy in the truth. [7] It is always ready to make allowances, to trust, to hope and to endure whatever comes. [8] Love never comes to an end. But if there are prophecies, they will be done away with; if tongues, they will fall silent; and if knowledge, it will be done away with. [9] For we know only imperfectly, and we prophesy imperfectly; [10] but once perfection comes, all imperfect things will be done away with. [11] When I was a child, I used to talk like a child, and see things as a child does, and think like a child; but now that I have become an adult, I have finished with all childish ways. [12] Now we see only reflections in a mirror, mere riddles, but then we shall be seeing face to face. Now I can know only imperfectly; but then I shall know just as fully as I am myself known. [13] As it is, these remain: faith, hope and love, the three of them; and the greatest of them is love.

*A window depicting the prophet Elijah by Richard Joseph King
in the Shrine of Saint Jude, Faversham, Kent.*

Reflection 3
<u>RESURRECTION OF THE WIDOW'S SON</u>
1 Kings 17:17-24

Invocation

Oh Merciful Father, you have a special care for the poor and those who suffer. Your prophet Elijah prayed to you for the life of the widow's son and he was heard. Accept now my plea for the presence of your Spirit during this time of prayer and also in my daily life, so that your Word may be always on my lips and in my heart. I make this prayer in the name of Christ our Lord. Amen.

Text

Read attentively the following text for the first time to understand the overall sense and to get the basic facts of the story.

[17] It happened after this that the son of the mistress of the house fell sick; his illness was so severe that in the end he expired. [18] And the woman said to Elijah, 'What quarrel have you with me, man of God? Have you come here to bring my sins home to me and to kill my son?' [19] 'Give me your son,' he said, and taking him from her lap he carried him to the upper room where he was staying and laid him on his bed. [20] He cried out to Yahweh, 'Yahweh my God, by killing her son do you mean to bring grief even to the widow who is looking after me?' [21] He stretched himself on the child three times and cried out to Yahweh, 'Yahweh my God, may the soul of this child, I beg you, come into him again!' [22] Yahweh heard Elijah's prayer and the child's soul came back into his body and he revived. [23] Elijah took the child, brought him down from the upper room into the house, and gave him to his mother. 'Look,' Elijah said, 'your son is alive.' [24] And the woman replied, 'Now I know you are a man of God and the word of Yahweh in your mouth is truth itself.'

Read

In this text we read about an even greater challenge for God. God has already provided food for Elijah by means of the ravens or the Arabs, and through the good offices of the widow, but now what can God do faced with death? Many ancient peoples thought that death was a god but this account shows that there is no God but the Lord. Truly God is the Lord of life!

This account was to enhance the reputation of the prophet and to establish the authority of his word. The widow interprets the death of her son according to the mentality which was prevalent also in New Testament times, that is, as a punishment for sins (cf. *John* 9:2). The widow thinks that the presence of the man of God has reminded God of her sins. Elijah stretches out over the boy. This gesture, analogous to those performed by the prophet Elisha (*2 Kings* 4:34) and by Saint Paul (*Acts* 20:10), symbolises the return of the life-giving power of God, the real worker of the miracle.

In the New Testament, the prophet Elijah is viewed as the precursor of Jesus. Explicitly and implicitly, the ministry of Elijah is seen as a model for the ministry of Jesus. As an example, see the miracle of Jesus when he raised the widow of Nain's son to life (*Luke* 7:11-17):

> [11] It happened that soon afterwards Jesus went to a town called Nain, accompanied by his disciples and a great number of people. [12] Now when he was near the gate of the town there was a dead man being carried out, the only son of his mother, and she was a widow. And a considerable number of the townspeople was with her. [13] When the Lord saw her he felt sorry for her and said to her, 'Don't cry.' [14] Then he went up and touched the bier and the bearers stood still, and he said, 'Young man, I tell you: get up.' [15] And the dead man sat up and began to talk, and Jesus gave him to his mother. [16] Everyone was filled with awe and glorified God saying, 'A great prophet has risen up among us; God has visited his people.' [17] And this view of him spread throughout Judaea and all over the countryside.

Reflect

Read the story from *1 Kings* 17:17-24 for a second time.

As an aid to reflection on this text, here are some questions. The underlying question is always: what does this text mean for me, or, what is God saying to me at this particular point in my life by means of this text?

1. Have you lost someone close to you? How has this affected your relationship with God?

2. Have you ever suffered from a grave illness and how did you relate to God during and after this experience?

3. What importance do you give to your sins and do you experience these as an impediment in your relationship with God?

4. Does your normal way of praying tell you something about your relationship with God? Do you think that you have a close relationship with God or a distant one?

5. Do you believe that your prayer has been heard and how did you feel when you received an answer from God?

6. Have you ever been in the presence of a friend of God? How did this experience affect you?

Respond

What response does your heart want to give to God? Perhaps a prayer from the Bible or the Christian Tradition will help. However it is also always good to use one's own words. Here is a prayer from the psalms (4:2-9):

> [2] When I call, answer me, God, upholder of my right. In my distress you have set me at large; take pity on me and hear my prayer! Children of men, how long will you be heavy of heart, why love what is vain and chase after illusions? [3] Realise that Yahweh performs wonders for his faithful, Yahweh listens when I call to him. [4] Be careful not to sin, speak in your hearts, and on your beds keep silence. [5] Loyally offer sacrifices, and trust in Yahweh. [6] Many keep saying, 'Who will put happiness before our eyes?' Let the light of your face shine on us. Yahweh, [7] to my heart you are a richer joy than all their corn and new wine. [8] In peace I lie down and at once fall asleep, for it is you and none other, Yahweh, who make me rest secure.

Rest

Continuing on the spiritual journey introduces us to a long process where God recreates us according to the image of the Son. The destruction of the "old self" is painful but the birth of the "new self" means that it was all worthwhile. If the cocoon or the egg could feel, they would certainly not want to be broken, but if they were not broken the butterfly or the bird would not be born. Another word for this process is *purification*. We are purified so that we can receive God, who desires to fill us with the divine life but we are too weak to receive this inestimable gift. Gradually God refines our spiritual senses in order to open us up to the divine life. On the spiritual journey there are highs and lows, times of light and times of shadow, times of strength and times of weakness. We must have patience and perseverance when God is putting the finishing touches to the masterpiece that is our life. Many artists do not like to reveal their work before it is finished. God acts in such a way with us. Normally we are not permitted to see what God is doing in our lives. The *prayer of silence* (see Appendix I) teaches us to leave space so that God can continue to work in us, trusting that the work of God's hands will be good. Looking upon creation, God saw that everything was good. (*Genesis* 1:31a).

As we let go of our own lives, we can rest in God and allow more space for the divine action. Gradually purification will take place in our lives. Inasmuch as we become more aware of the presence and action of God in our lives as the source of all happiness, we become more ready to dismantle the *false self* that we now perceive as a great burden. In the false self we have placed our hope of happiness, and now, little by little, there is developing a gradual self-forgetfulness and a progressive self-abandonment, trusting in the power of God to lead us to the fullness of human life. All our likes, dislikes and desires gradually merge into a radical submission to the will of God, not only during prayer but also in the whole of life.

Our ideas, opinions and words normally back up our false ego and we use these to convince ourselves that we are right in every situation. There is a time when it is good to leave aside our words, even the most beautiful, and our thoughts, even the holiest. It is difficult however to remain in silence without thinking of something in particular. The method of prayer presented in Appendix I can help us remain in silence and not follow every distraction. Silence can be empty and this has no particular Christian meaning, but silence can also be full of meaning if there exists a desire in the person to be in the presence of God and to consent to God's purifying and transforming action in everyday life.

When we attempt to remain in silence for a time we are immediately subject to distractions. In the *prayer in secret*, we use a sacred word to turn the heart towards God when we become aware that we are thinking of something else.[18] Prayer in secret is a prayer of intention and not of attention, in the sense that it is the will that counts and not the imagination. It is important not to judge one's own prayer. If one tries to pray with a good motive, that wants to be in God's presence and open to the divine action, this is true prayer, even if one feels that it has been a complete waste of time. God can use your desire for your spiritual health. Only God can judge the human heart and only God can judge whether what we are doing is really prayer.

I suggest that you take a look at the first Appendix for the simple guidelines for the prayer in secret and try to spend twenty minutes or so in silence. If you find yourself thinking about something, simply turn your heart once again towards God with a *sacred word*, which is a short word, sacred for you, that acts as a symbol of your intention to be in the presence of God and of your consent to the divine action in your life.

Act

Below you will find suggestions from the Bible text of some phrases that you can take with you throughout the day as a reminder of the presence of God, but whatever speaks strongly to you is always better.

"Man of God?"

"He called on the Lord"

"Yahweh, my God"

"I beg you"

"your son is alive"

"the Word of God is truth"

"Yahweh heard his prayer"

A good tree produces good fruit. If we are faithful to the practice of prayer as a relationship with God, it will produce good fruit in our life. Often during prayer we experience nothing but we must listen and be awake for the activity of God in all the events of life. In the story of the resurrection of the widow's son, the

---

18 For the concept of the "sacred word" in this method of prayer, see especially Thomas Keating, *Open Mind, Open Heart*, chapter 5, and Elizabeth Smith & Joseph Chalmers, *A Deeper Love*, p. 36-53.

prophet Elijah prays with great fervour for the young man. Is there someone you should remember especially today? Carry this person (or these people) in your heart throughout the day and remember to pray for them. Remember that God is very near and always hears you.

> If anyone loves me, he will keep my word and the Father will love him and we will come and make our home with him. (*John* 14:23).

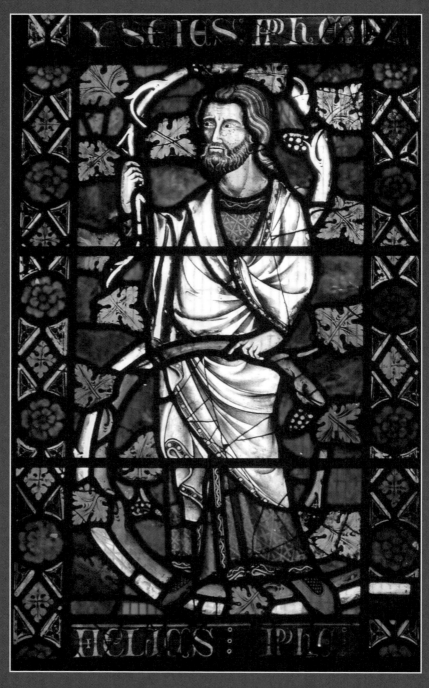

Elijah depicted in a medieval stained glass 'Tree of Jesse' window in the Church of Saint Mary in Shrewsbury.

Reflection 4
<u>THE MEETING BETWEEN ELIJAH AND OBADIAH</u>
1 Kings **18:1-16**

Invocation

Father, by the power of your Spirit you hid your prophet Elijah from his enemies. In the fullness of time, you sent Elijah to speak your Word. You found Obadiah, a man faithful to you, to help the prophet Elijah fulfil your will. Help me, Father, to be open to your Word and fill me with your Spirit so that I may always do what is pleasing to you. I make this prayer to you, Father, through Jesus Christ your Son, by the power of the Holy Spirit. Amen.

Text

Read attentively the following text for the first time in order to understand the sense and to get the basic facts of the story.

[1] A long time went by, and the word of Yahweh came to Elijah in the third year, 'Go, present yourself to Ahab, and I will send rain on the country.' [2] So Elijah set off to present himself to Ahab. As the famine was particularly severe in Samaria, [3] Ahab summoned Obadiah, the master of the palace – Obadiah held Yahweh in great reverence: [4] when Jezebel was butchering the prophets of Yahweh, Obadiah took a hundred of them and hid them, fifty at a time, in a cave, and kept them provided with food and water – [5] and Ahab said to Obadiah, 'Come along, we must scour the country, all the springs and all the ravines in the hope of finding grass to keep horses and mules alive, or we shall have to slaughter some of our stock.' [6] They divided the country for the purpose of their survey; Ahab went one way by himself and Obadiah went another way by himself. [7] While Obadiah was on his way, whom should he meet but Elijah. Recognising him he fell on his face and said, 'So it is you, my lord Elijah!' [8] 'Yes,' he replied, 'go and tell your master, "Elijah is here." ' [9] But Obadiah said, 'What sin have I committed, for you to put your servant into Ahab's power and cause my death?

[10] As Yahweh your God lives, there is no nation or kingdom where my master has not sent in search of you; and when they said, "He is not there," he made the kingdom or nation swear an oath that they did not know where you were. [11] And now you say to me, "Go and tell your master: Elijah is here." [12] But as soon as I leave you, the spirit of Yahweh will carry you away and I shall not know where; I shall go and tell Ahab; he will not be able to find you, and then he will kill me. Yet from his youth your servant has revered Yahweh. [13] Has no one told my lord what I did when Jezebel butchered the prophets of Yahweh, how I hid a hundred of them in a cave, fifty at a time, and kept them provided with food and water? [14] And now you say to me, "Go and tell your master: Elijah is here." Why, he will kill me!' [15] Elijah replied, 'As Yahweh Sabaoth lives, whom I serve, I shall present myself to him today!' [16] Obadiah went to find Ahab and tell him the news, and Ahab then went to find Elijah.

Read

There is a general agreement among scholars that the stories about Elijah-Obadiah and Elijah-Ahab are quite distinct, but there is no agreement as to where exactly the text should be divided. For the purposes of our prayer, I have divided the text after verse 16.

In the third year of the famine, Elijah was sent by God to announce the end of the drought to Ahab (v.1). The prophet presents himself to Obadiah, the master of the royal palace. He is a follower of Yahweh (in fact his name means "servant of Yahweh") and he had hidden many prophets from the persecution of Jezebel (v.3-4). Elijah commands Obadiah to call the king, but Obadiah is frightened because he knows that Elijah appears and disappears by the power of the spirit of Yahweh. Other cases in which the divine spirit transports a prophet are recorded in *Ezekiel* 8:3, 11:1, 43:5; *Acts* 8:39. Only when Elijah promises to remain does Obadiah obey (v.15-16).

The drought has gone on for a long time. However, according to the way of counting at the time, probably not more than 13 or 14 months passed. Baal, the god of storms and rain, could do nothing! The writer wants to show that the rain depends totally on the word of Yahweh, the true God.

Twice the text says that Obadiah, an important man, and at the same time faithful to God, was a God-fearer. It is important to note that the fear of God, mentioned often in the Bible, does not refer to the feeling of fear. This feeling is a defence mechanism that pumps adrenalin into the body to combat whatever we feel is threatening us. It also gives us the push to run away in order to avoid the danger. Certainly these reactions are not recommended in the relationship with God. We are God's children and Jesus has revealed the God of the Old Testament as our Father who loves us deeply. The *fear of God* refers to a right relationship between the human person and God. We are children of God but at the same time we are creatures, and we must respect and obey the divine commandments that are given to us as guidelines for a happy life here on earth and in the life to come. The fear of God in the biblical sense implies having a true image of God, and also a true love towards God, which must be incarnated in life.

In this story there is a great famine but the king is more preoccupied with his animals than worrying about the effects on the people. The army and the men of power used the animals. Ahab is more interested in his own power than in helping the people. Obadiah wants to help Elijah but only reluctantly and secretly. Elijah wants Obadiah to announce to the king "Elijah is here" but the Hebrew can also mean, "Behold, the Lord is my God". Obadiah does not want to make this announcement to the king because he is afraid. This story anticipates the accusation made by Elijah to the people on Mount Carmel that they wanted to have two gods (*1 Kings* 18:21). In the life of faith there are always temptations to be less than totally faithful.

The fear of Obadiah in regard to Ahab is a reflection of the change which had taken place in Israel where the power over life and death rested on royal whim. In verse 15 God is given the title "Lord of hosts" and this title is very frequent in prophetic literature. The title can be understood in various ways but here it seems that it refers to the omnipotence of God.

Reflect

Read again the story in *1 Kings* 18:1-16.

To assist your reflection here are some questions:

1. The word of God was addressed to Elijah. Is God speaking to you? How? What is God saying to you at this time in your life?

2. Is God calling you to do something?

3. What does rain symbolise for you?

4. Where is there a famine of God's word now and what can be done in the situation?

5. Obadiah was a God fearer and he showed his love for God with good works. What is the evidence of your relationship with God?

6. Obadiah was afraid to carry out the command of the prophet Elijah but he did it in the end. What do you feel, faced with what you believe is the will of God for you?

Respond

What is your response to the Word of God? It is always good to use your own words but a prayer from the Bible (*Psalm* 2) might help.

> [1] Why this uproar among the nations, this impotent muttering of the peoples? [2] Kings of the earth take up position, princes plot together against Yahweh and his anointed, [3] 'Now let us break their fetters! Now let us throw off their bonds!' [4] He who is enthroned in the heavens laughs, Yahweh makes a mockery of them, [5] then in his anger rebukes them, in his rage he strikes them with terror. [6] 'I myself have anointed my king on Zion my holy mountain.' [7] I will proclaim the decree of Yahweh: He said to me, 'You are my son, today have I fathered you. [8] Ask of me, and I shall give you the nations as your birthright, the whole wide world as your possession. [9] With an iron sceptre you will break them, shatter them like so many pots.' [10] So now, you kings, come to your senses, you earthly rulers, learn your lesson! [11] In fear be submissive to Yahweh; [12] with trembling kiss his feet, lest he be angry and your way come to nothing, for his fury flares up in a moment. How blessed are all who take refuge in him!

Leave a space so that your heart can speak freely to God.

Rest

We all need some space in our frenetic modern life for silence – not only exterior but also interior. I have already offered a method of prayer in the first Appendix, which can help us wait for God in silence. This is a prayer of silence or desire, or prayer in secret, according to the words of Jesus in Saint Matthew's Gospel (6:6):

> When you pray, go to your private room, shut yourself in, and so pray to your Father who is in that secret place, and your Father who sees all that is done in secret will reward you.

The silence is an integral part of *Lectio Divina* but it is always difficult to maintain a silence that produces fruit in daily life. While the prayer in secret, described in the Appendix, is not part of *Lectio Divina* in the strict sense, it can help it move towards its goal. The prayer described in the Appendix consists simply in being before God with empty hands, desiring God's presence and action in our lives. The goal of all prayer is contemplation, not in the sense of having mystical experiences, but in the sense of an intimate transformation of the human heart. *Lectio Divina* as practiced by the ancient monks moves naturally towards silence, which, with the grace of God, becomes contemplation when and how God wishes. Our brains are different from the ancients and it is very difficult for us to close ourselves off from external and internal noise, which distracts us from simply being in the presence of God who loves us so much and wants to transform us so that we will be capable to receive the divine life. For this reason, a method for remaining in silence is very useful. Using a method like the one suggested in the Appendix does not mean that we will cease to have distractions but we will have a method to combat them. Combating distractions is not the correct phrase because it is not necessary; let every thought come and go without resisting it and without becoming disturbed no matter how many thoughts you have. Simply remain in silence in the presence of God.

In the silence, the heart remains awake and beseeches God to transform it. Contemplation is a process in which we are brought to transformation when we can see with the eyes of God and love with God's own heart.

Now put the book down and also leave aside the text of Scripture so that you can simply be in the presence of God in silence. If you choose to use the method that I have suggested, when you become aware that you are thinking about something, return your heart to God ever so gently by the use of the *sacred word*, which is the symbol of your intention to be in the presence of God and to consent to the divine action in your life.

Act

True Christian prayer must be incarnated in life and therefore it is useful to find some method for extending one's prayer into the events of every day. This helps us remember the presence of God outside the time of prayer and therefore helps us do God's will. Christian prayer must have some effect on daily life; if it does not, we must examine why. The *false self* can instrumentalise prayer in order to assure itself of the esteem of other people or to feel holy and secure in the sight of God. The struggle against the false self endures for the whole of life and one weapon in this battle is prayer. Saint Paul (*Ephesians* 6:13-17) gives us a description of the armour of the spiritual person:

> [13] That is why you must take up all God's armour, or you will not be able to put up any resistance on the evil day, or stand your ground even though you exert yourselves to the full. [14] So stand your ground, with truth a belt round your waist, and uprightness a breastplate, [15] wearing for shoes on your feet the eagerness to spread the gospel of peace [16] and always carrying the shield of faith so that you can use it to quench the burning arrows of the Evil One. [17] And then you must take salvation as your helmet and the sword of the Spirit, that is, the word of God.

One way of extending *Lectio Divina* into everyday life is to choose some word either from the text being reflected upon or from the whole of your relationship with God that has gone before. I can suggest some words or phrases from the text we have been using.

"the Word of Yahweh"

"I will send rain"

"held Yahweh in great reverence"

"What sin have I committed?"

"Yahweh your God lives"

"the spirit of Yahweh"

"your servant has revered Yahweh"

In our text, Obadiah finally does the will of God that came to him by means of the words of the Prophet Elijah. Certainly God will speak to you in several ways. Try to be attentive to what God is saying to you today.

Elijah window at Terenure College, Dublin.

Reflection 5
<u>ELIJAH AND AHAB</u>
1 Kings **18:17-19**

Invocation

Oh Father, by means of your prophet Elijah, you revealed the unfaithfulness of Ahab. Help me to be always faithful and send your Spirit into my heart so that I can hear your voice and that your Word may transform my life. Through Christ our Lord. Amen.

Text

Read attentively the following text for the first time in order to capture the sense and to get the basic facts of the story.

> [17] When he saw Elijah, Ahab said, 'So there you are, you scourge of Israel!' [18] 'Not I,' he replied, 'I am not the scourge of Israel, you and your family are; because you have deserted Yahweh and followed Baal. [19] Now give orders for all Israel to gather round me on Mount Carmel, and also the four hundred prophets of Baal who eat at Jezebel's table.'

Read

Finally Elijah and Ahab meet. The king accuses the prophet of being the scourge of Israel (v.17). Probably the king wanted to say that Elijah has made Baal angry and so the idol has not sent rain but Elijah returns the accusation to Ahab. It is the king and his family who have brought many problems on Israel because they have forgotten the commandments of Yahweh and they have followed the baals (v.18). The word *baals* is in the plural because there are many manifestations of the Baal of Canaan. Elijah wants to prove who is God in Israel. He tells Ahab to call all Israel to witness a contest with the prophets of Baal on Mount Carmel (v.19). For Elijah this is an "either – or" contest. Either Yahweh or Baal is God in Israel; there is no room for both.

Reflect

Read the text of *1 Kings* 18:17-19 for a second time.

To assist your reflection on this text and to help bring the text closer to your life experience, there follows some questions.

1. Ahab says that Elijah is the scourge of Israel. A holy person is not always comfortable because he or she shows up the lack of depth of other people. Have you ever met someone who is truly holy? How have you felt in the presence of such a person?

2. Elijah revealed the unfaithfulness of Ahab. In what ways are you unfaithful to God?

3. If you are aware of some infidelity or sin, what are you going to do about it? What more can you do in order to grow in your relationship with God?

4. The Prophet Elijah mentioned the 400 prophets of Baal who ate at the expense of Jezebel. There is always a temptation to give up one's principles for the sake of security. Are your principles untouchable?

According to the *Second Letter of Timothy* (3:16-17):

> All scripture is inspired by God and useful for refuting error, for guiding people's lives and teaching them to be upright. This is how someone who is dedicated to God becomes fully equipped and ready for any good work.

The story of the meeting between Elijah and Ahab is very short. Have you found something in this story that can help you?

Respond

Read again the text *1 Kings* 18:17-19 to listen to what God is saying to you.

The Prophet Elijah seems to be full of trust in God. Do you have trust in God? Have a word with God now. Perhaps you would like to pray for a greater trust or perhaps for forgiveness? There follows a prayer from the *Psalms* (16:7-11) that might help you.

> [7] I bless Yahweh who is my counsellor; even at night my heart instructs me. [8] I keep Yahweh before me always, for with him at my

right hand, nothing can shake me. [9] So my heart rejoices, my soul delights, my body too will rest secure, [10] for you will not abandon me to Sheol, you cannot allow your faithful servant to see the abyss. [11] You will teach me the path of life, unbounded joy in your presence, at your right hand delight for ever.

Rest

Contemplation is a process of growth that requires our faithfulness and co-operation. The ways of the Lord are not our ways and so we are invited to begin a journey into the unknown. It is unknown but we can name the terminus of the journey, that is, that we become one with Christ!

Contemplation is above all a way of faith. We cannot judge this way with our ordinary senses because faith goes beyond our human ways of judging. The only way to judge whether contemplation truly is an encounter with God is by its fruits, that is, its effects in our daily life.

During deep prayer we let go of our own interests as we enter into God's world, and little by little we take on ourselves the mind of Christ:

> [5] Make your own the mind of Christ Jesus: [6] Who, being in the form of God, did not count equality with God something to be grasped. [7] But he emptied himself, taking the form of a slave, becoming as human beings are; and being in every way like a human being, [8] he was humbler yet, even to accepting death, death on a cross. [9] And for this God raised him high, and gave him the name which is above all other names; [10] so that all beings in the heavens, on earth and in the underworld, should bend the knee at the name of Jesus [11] and that every tongue should acknowledge Jesus Christ as Lord, to the glory of God the Father. (*Philippians* 2:5-11)

This leads us to the virtue of detachment, which means to be in a right relationship with everyone and everything. According to Saint John of the Cross and Saint Teresa of Avila, detachment is one of the most important virtues of the Christian life.[19] Often we define ourselves by our role: teacher, housewife, religious sister, priest and so on. If we perceive that something is threatening this role, it can be a threat to our whole personality, to our whole world.

Detachment means that gradually we become free from disordered attachments to people and to things in order that we might obtain the freedom of the children

---

19   *Way of Perfection*, 8; *Dark Night*, 12.

of God, and so that others can also be free. The word "things" includes many different realities. It includes material things, ideas, feelings, emotions, etc. Material things are good and have been created for the use of everyone but it is very easy to let things enslave our hearts. Saint John of the Cross wrote: "It matters little whether the thread that ties the bird is fine or thick, because it still remains tied until the thread is broken. It is true that the fine thread can be broken more easily; but if it is not broken, the bird cannot fly."[20]

When we are too close to material things they can blind us to reality, but when there is a distance between things and us we can see them in a true light and appreciate them for what they are. We must also look to our feelings and emotions. It is not good to ignore them but if they drive us and control us, we are not free. Suppression of emotions and feelings is very dangerous and ultimately senseless because they will continue to emerge in some way until we attend to what they are telling us. A faithful commitment to prayer helps us to become free in relation to our emotions. Gradually God can reveal our "hidden agenda", that is, what truly motivates us often without us being aware. We might like to think that our motives are always Christian but the truth is often something else.

There is a tendency within us to try to possess other people. There is also a tendency to turn people into things in order to feed our needs. Our call is to love others as God loves them because divine love is liberating. People are liberated to become themselves whether this happens to please us or not. As we entrust ourselves to God at various levels of our personality, we can begin to give life to others.

Detachment does not mean rejecting or despising things, and much less people, in case they in some way damage our precious relationship with God. This would be neither Christian nor human. It does not mean denying that we have certain emotions, or trying to repress them because we think that they cannot possibly form part of the image we have of ourselves. This does not help us at all. Feelings and emotions are neither good nor bad. We must accept them as part of ourselves. Perhaps they are a part that we would prefer not to recognise but nevertheless they are an important part. By means of a personal relationship with God, prayer helps me to accept myself as I am, in the same way that God accepts me. If God had wished us to be angels, we would have been created as such. The Son of God became one of us so that God might experience what it means to be human. We insult God if we try to attempt to repress our human

---

20 *Ascent of Mount Carmel*, I, 11, 4.

nature, but we are called to move towards maturity, which means to become fully human and fully alive.

There are certain stages of human development through which we must pass. Human growth does not stop when we become physically adult, but the process goes on at least until death. An important part of human growth is the so-called "spiritual life". There are various stages of development of the Christian life. We can read about the great saints and perhaps wish to become like them but we are called to be saints in our own way through our humanity. We are called to show forth the image of God in which we have been created. Each one of us possesses a unique gift to reveal a particular facet of God by means of our personality. We cannot become saints in a day. There is a long road to the perfection of our humanity. The Exodus is a good model for the journey that each one of us must undertake. The Israelites were forty years in the desert before they were allowed into the Promised Land. We need a bit of patience with the process and above all with ourselves.

We cannot pass from one stage of growth to another until we have dealt with what needs to be dealt with at each point. However, a time comes when we must continue and not delay. What is good at one moment can become an obstacle at another time. As Saint Paul says, "When I was a child, I used to talk like a child, and see things as a child does, and think like a child; but now that I have become an adult, I have finished with all childish ways." (*1 Corinthians* 13:11) We must abandon what does not help at the right moment. Leaving behind many things that have been important to us can be painful, but it is necessary so that we can continue the journey not overloaded with too much unnecessary baggage.

Spontaneously our tendency is to grasp on to people and things thinking that these will bring us happiness. However at some point in life we will discover that this is not true. With the help of a faithful and committed prayer we discover that only God can respond to the desires of our heart. God is the source and the goal of all our desires. Gradually we arrive at the understanding that only God can totally satisfy us. A powerful model for a truly free individual is Saint Francis of Assisi who loved the whole of creation with a great passion but, because of his love for God, Francis was not enslaved by anything.

Slowly but surely, in the manner that we grow in our relationship with God, we can let go of our obvious attachments, but then we must deal with the more subtle attachments. In the same way that we can grasp on to material things or people, we can also grasp on to 'religious' things and even to spiritual feelings.

Prayer in secret, a method which can be found in the first Appendix, helps us to let go control when it comes to prayer. At first letting go control will not be altogether pleasing because we like having control of what is happening, but as we let go control we discover that we are in safe hands, that is, in the hands of God. On the way we will need to confront various temptations that are subtle ways of taking back control from God.

Leave aside your words, ideas, opinions, thoughts, and leave a bit of space for God to speak to your heart. To help you remain watchful in the silence, I suggest the so-called *prayer in secret*, which you can find explained in the first Appendix. The only real distraction in this kind of prayer is if you get up and leave before the end of the time you have decided to dedicate to it. All thoughts, even the most interesting, are not necessarily distractions. Resist no thought; retain no thought; react to no thought; when you become aware of being distracted, simply return ever so gently to your sacred word as the symbol of your intention to remain in the presence of God and to be open to the divine action.

Act

Choose a word or a phrase from the text or from your own reflection and ongoing relationship with God to extend your prayer into daily life. I am not suggesting any particular word or phrase from the text we have been using in this chapter.

Any method of prayer is useful inasmuch as it helps us to grow in our relationship with God. If this relationship is in fact growing, it will affect every aspect of life. *Prayer in secret* is not simply a method of prayer that one uses once or twice a day; it is a spiritual discipline and the method is only a part. First of all, this *prayer in secret* does not substitute for all your other ways of relating to God. We must continue to develop our relationship with God in whatever way we can, using whatever helps us. It would be normal that a faithful practice of the *prayer in secret* would help us appreciate more profoundly our traditional devotions. The *prayer in secret* comes from the tradition of *Lectio Divina*, and goes very well with a regular practice of reading Holy Scripture. It helps us enter more deeply into the Scriptures and helps us to see them from another point of view. The Scriptures are not just stories about long-dead people; they are the Word of God for each one of us at this very moment. When we do not have much time, we can pick up the Gospels and take a word or a phrase to carry with us during the day. When we listen to God in the silence of our heart, we become more aware that God is actually speaking to us in the Scriptures. To make sure that the silence is not empty, we must not neglect the nourishment that God provides for us during the day.

It is very important that we are faithful to the daily encounter with God. Many people say that they just have no time for prayer. This can be true but often these words simply tell others of the priorities of the speaker. We make sure that we have time for what we want to do. Perhaps it is true that we do not have much time for prayer but it does not really need much time. Normally, for a method like that of the *prayer in secret*, the recommended time is 20 minutes twice a day.

One can only do what is possible. Prayer is our response to God's initiative. God has no need of time but we do. God can do wonders without us but normally God seeks our co-operation. When we give time to God, we are showing that we are taking the spiritual journey seriously. We must be creative to find opportunities to be with God and we must be creative in how we use these opportunities. What is really important is our intention. If we truly desire that God take possession of our hearts, we must seek to make this desire a reality by living a God-centred existence, and if we accept the consequences, then all will be well. It is not possible to be more generous than God.

Spiritual formation is also important. It seems that today some people prefer a religion in which they can choose the bits they like. The spiritual formation of many Christians seems limited to what they have learned in school and the Sunday sermon. The practice of the *prayer in secret* comes out of the Christian contemplative tradition. When a person starts a practice like this, he or she often wants to learn more about this tradition. The Christian contemplative tradition contains the wisdom of centuries and the experience of the great saints. It is open to those who have eyes to see and ears to hear and those who wish to learn more about their faith. To have a profound relationship with God, it is not necessary to have great intelligence or education, but culpable ignorance cannot be considered a virtue.

Try to listen to your heart throughout the day. What is really important for you? Are you really seeking only God or are there other "gods" in your life?

Moses (left) and Elijah (right) in a sixteenth-century window from the Carmelite church in Antwerp, now in Saint George's Church, Hanover Square, London.

Reflection 6
THE CHALLENGE ON MOUNT CARMEL I
1 Kings **18:20-29**

Invocation

Oh God, your prophet Elijah had a great trust in you. In the power of your Spirit, Elijah challenged the people to choose whom they wished to follow, either you my God, or an empty idol. Save me from all the modern idols and help me to be always faithful to you, oh Father. Send your Holy Spirit to fill my heart with your wisdom, so that I will choose in every circumstance of my life whatever is in conformity with your will. I make this humble prayer in the name of Christ, your Son and my Lord. Amen.

Text

Read attentively the following text for the first time in order to understand the overall sense, and to grasp the basic facts of the story.

[20] Ahab called all Israel together and assembled the prophets on Mount Carmel. [21] Elijah stepped out in front of all the people. 'How long', he said, 'do you mean to hobble first on one leg then on the other? If Yahweh is God, follow him; if Baal, follow him.' But the people had nothing to say. [22] Elijah then said to them, 'I, I alone, am left as a prophet of Yahweh, while the prophets of Baal are four hundred and fifty. [23] Let two bulls be given us; let them choose one for themselves, dismember it but not set fire to it. I in my turn shall prepare the other bull, but not set fire to it. [24] You must call on the name of your god, and I shall call on the name of Yahweh; the god who answers with fire, is God indeed.' The people all answered, 'Agreed!' [25] Elijah then said to the prophets of Baal, 'Choose one bull and begin, for there are more of you. Call on the name of your god but light no fire.' [26] They took the bull and prepared it, and from morning to midday they called on the name of Baal. 'O Baal, answer us!' they cried, but there was no voice, no answer, as they performed their hobbling dance round the altar which they had

made. [27] Midday came, and Elijah mocked them. 'Call louder,' he said, 'for he is a god: he is preoccupied or he is busy, or he has gone on a journey; perhaps he is asleep and needs to be woken up!' [28] So they shouted louder and gashed themselves, as their custom was, with swords and spears until the blood flowed down them. [29] Midday passed, and they ranted on until the time when the offering is presented; but there was no voice, no answer, no sign of attention.

Read

From the 15th century before Christ, Carmel was considered sacred. Carmel was just the place for the story contained in *1 Kings* 18, which asks, "Who is the ruler?" "Who is Lord?" "Who gives the rain?" This contest between Elijah and the prophets of Baal was very important in the history of Israel. The prophets of Baal used every part of their armoury to call on their god but without success. In ancient societies dancing was an important religious expression (see *Psalm* 26:6). The reason that the prophets cut themselves and shed blood was to make their prayer more urgent and more effective. Shedding blood during prayer was prohibited according to Jewish law (*Deuteronomy* 14:1; *Leviticus* 19:28), but occasionally was practiced (*Jeremiah* 41:5), and it was normal in other ancient religions. The idea was to lose self-control in order to leave space for an invasion of the divine, considered indispensable to obtain what one sought in prayer.

Elijah offered to those who opposed him the choice of the sacrificial bull and also the first appeal to their god (v.25). They performed their rituals but without success and this caused the scorn of Elijah to fall on them (v.27).

Reflect

Read the text again in order to enter more profoundly into the Word of God. To assist your reflection here are some questions.

1. What melody do you follow: God's or your own?

2. Is there some infidelity in your life that prevents you from making a complete act of trust in God? Do you confuse God with certain religious practices or superstitions?

3. The people say nothing when the prophet Elijah challenges them. What is your reaction when faced with the first two

questions? Is there a resistance within you at the implication that your relationship with God perhaps is not deep?

4. On Mount Carmel, the Prophet Elijah was opposed by 450 prophets of Baal. Our modern society does not support the search for a profound relationship with God. How do you feel faced with the challenges of our society against the faith?

Respond

Give yourself a bit of space so that your heart has time to open itself to God. What do you want to say to God? Do you want to pray for a stronger faith? A deeper personal relationship with God? Forgiveness for having followed another melody to that proposed by Christ in the Gospel? Open your heart to God. Perhaps the following prayer from *Psalm* 23 (1-6) will help you.

> [1] Yahweh is my shepherd, I lack nothing. [2] In grassy meadows he lets me lie. By tranquil streams he leads me [3] to restore my spirit. He guides me in paths of saving justice as befits his name. [4] Even were I to walk in a ravine as dark as death I should fear no danger, for you are at my side. Your staff and your crook are there to soothe me. [5] You prepare a table for me under the eyes of my enemies; you anoint my head with oil; my cup brims over. [6] Kindness and faithful love pursue me every day of my life. I make my home in the house of Yahweh for all time to come.

Rest

At the beginning of a serious and profound relationship with God, it is normal that prayer comes easily and gives a sense of closeness with God. However, normally not much time passes before the individual enters into a dry period when prayer becomes difficult and very challenging. There is the feeling of wasting time, and often there is the temptation to leave prayer in order to give more time for good works, or to leave prayer completely because one feels no sense of progress. I have already said that these stages are very normal but God is always completely free and can act outside these norms. However, the Christian tradition, with many centuries of experience behind it, suggests that some stages of the spiritual life, or the spiritual journey, appear with a certain frequency in the life of Christians to make it possible to say that these stages are "normal".

The Carmelite tradition is particularly rich in the area of the human-divine relationship. A certain dryness in prayer is normal but also can be one of the signs that, according to Saint John of the Cross, suggest that the person is passing through the first part of the dark night, that is the movement from meditation to contemplation in the classic sense.[21] Normally the help of a spiritual director with experience of the contemplative way is necessary to discern this movement.

In the midst of dryness when it seems that we are receiving nothing from God, and a holy thought enters our head during prayer, it is understandable that we try to grasp hold of this thought and chew on it till nothing remains like a dog with a bone. However, at this point it is better to let go of all thoughts, whether they are holy or not, because they are not sufficient to nourish us. Saint John of the Cross writes of the baby who is fed with milk but as the baby grows, milk is no longer sufficient; the child needs more substantial food.[22]

One might ask: why not welcome the good and holy thoughts and other divine inspirations? My first response is: how do you know which inspiration or thought comes from God? If something is really from God, it will return at the appropriate time. During the *prayer in secret*, your silence, both external and internal, is much more eloquent than many words or thoughts. In the silence you can collect up all your intentions and inspirations without reflecting on them.

To the first question of the prophet Elijah about whom they should follow, the people answered not even a word. At the challenge of the prophet to have a contest between God and Baal, the people answered, "Agreed!" There is a right time to speak and a right time for silence. At times we remain silent when we should speak but more often we speak when it would be better to remain silent. Now take some time for silence. Saint John of the Cross wrote that the language God best understands is silent love.[23] In the silence we can simply be before God with our love and our desire, awaiting the divine response. God is totally free but cannot resist a soul that is humble and, aware of its own poverty, waits in silence.

I invite you now to enter into a period of silence. In order to receive the benefit of the silence, I suggest at least twenty minutes and you can find the method for the *prayer in secret* in the first Appendix to help you remain in silence.

---

21 Cf. *Ascent of Mount Carmel*, II, 13,2-4 and *Dark Night*, I, 9.
22 *Dark Night*, I,1.
23 *Maxims & Counsels*, 53.

Act

How does one hear and continue faithful to the melody of God in the midst of the noise of daily life? This is the great challenge of the Christian life. Celebrating the Eucharist and the sacrament of reconciliation frequently is a great help to remain faithful because we always need the grace of God. Certainly God is always present to us but we are not always present to God. We must do what we can in prayer to help increase our love. A challenge is to find a method for remaining always in the presence of God in the midst of all the things that we simply have to do. Obviously you cannot always think about God because you must think of so many other things but a deep and growing relationship does not need many words or great thoughts.

Think about some good relationship you have in your life (husband, wife, friend). How do you manage to keep this relationship in good shape in today's frenetic pace? Is there anything you can learn from this relationship to help you grow in your relationship with God? During the day give thanks to God for the special people in your life and pray for them. Throughout the day make little acts of faith in God – Father, Son and Holy Spirit.

The prophet Elijah depicted in the Carmelite habit,
whose 'word burned like a torch' (Sirach 48:1).
Window at C.I.S.A. (International Centre of Saint Albert), Rome.

Reflection 7
THE CHALLENGE ON MOUNT CARMEL II
1 Kings 18:30-39

Invocation

Oh Father, you gave a great faith to your prophet Elijah. Because of a wonderful manifestation of your creative and redemptive power, the people answered, "Yahweh is God! Yahweh is God!" Still in our own days you show your almighty power but often the modern world does not know how to discern the signs of your presence and action. Help me to be aware of your presence in my life and in the world. Send me your Spirit so that I can live as you wish and be open in prayer to your plans. Through Christ our Lord. Amen.

Text

Read attentively the following text for the first time in order to capture the sense and the basic facts of the story.

[30] Then Elijah said to all the people, 'Come over to me,' and all the people came over to him. He repaired Yahweh's altar which had been torn down. [31] Elijah took twelve stones, corresponding to the number of tribes of the sons of Jacob, to whom the word of Yahweh had come, 'Israel is to be your name,' [32] and built an altar in the name of Yahweh. Round the altar he dug a trench of a size to hold two measures of seed. [33] He then arranged the wood, dismembered the bull, and laid it on the wood. [34] Then he said, 'Fill four jars with water and pour it on the burnt offering and on the wood.' They did this. He said, 'Do it a second time;' they did it a second time. He said, 'Do it a third time;' they did it a third time. [35] The water flowed round the altar until even the trench itself was full of water. [36] At the time when the offering is presented, Elijah the prophet stepped forward. 'Yahweh, God of Abraham, Isaac and Israel,' he said, 'let them know today that you are God in Israel, and that I am your servant, that I have done all these things at your command. [37] Answer me, Yahweh, answer me, so that this people may know that

you, Yahweh, are God and are winning back their hearts.' [38] Then Yahweh's fire fell and consumed the burnt offering and the wood and licked up the water in the trench. [39] When all the people saw this they fell on their faces. 'Yahweh is God,' they cried, 'Yahweh is God!'

Read

Elijah repaired the altar that was probably an ancient altar to Yahweh (v.30) and he prepared it for the sacrifice. This symbolises the infidelity of the people toward their God because the altar had to be rebuilt.

In the Bible, fire is a sign of the presence of Yahweh (*Exodus* 3:2), protecting (*Zechariah* 2:5), purifying (*Malachi* 3:2) and punishing (*Leviticus* 20:14). The fire that consumes the offering of Elijah is the lightning that announces the rain (*Judges* 6:21, 13:20; *Ezekiel* 1:13; *Job* 1:16; *2 Kings* 1:10-14). The lightning was not something to fear but a reminder that Yahweh was present to protect his people and punish their enemies. Lightning is the fire of God ("es elohim" in Hebrew) and Elijah is the man of God ("is elohim" in Hebrew). The prophet is a man so close to God that he can use God's lightning.

Elijah put water on the altar (v.34-35) to show perhaps that he was not employing any tricks, and also to show his total trust in the God of Israel. He prayed to Yahweh who, in answer, sent lightning from heaven and burnt up the sacrifice of Elijah (v.26-38). Lightning was the special weapon of Baal but here Yahweh produces it at the appropriate moment. The people were profoundly struck and put their heads to the ground crying out, "Yahweh is God" (v.39). This cry is the echo of Elijah's name.

We cannot know precisely what happened on Mount Carmel but that something tremendous took place is certain. If Jezebel persecuted the prophets of Yahweh and actively promoted the cult of Baal and maintained a great number of prophets at court, something drastic must have happened to control this movement before the death of Ahab.

Reflect

Read the text for a second time in order to enter more profoundly into the Word of God. To help your reflection, I have suggested some questions.

1. The Prophet Elijah reminds the people of the foundations of their religion with his preparations for the sacrifice. Do you know well the foundations of the Christian faith? If not, what do you intend to do about it? If you think you know your faith, are you sure?

2. Elijah reconstructed the altar of the Lord that had been demolished. Saint Francis of Assisi received the command of God to repair the Church. What is your reaction to the Church: to build it up or tear it down?

3. In his prayer of offering, the prophet Elijah spoke to the "God of Abraham, of Isaac and of Israel". Jesus Christ revealed that this God was his Father and also ours. What is your concept of God and how does this concept influence your life?

4. Elijah did everything according to the will of God. How specifically do you accomplish the will of God?

5. Elijah prayed, "Answer me, Yahweh, answer me". Do you think that God hears your prayer and how does God respond?

6. Elijah prayed that God convert the heart of the people. Is there a part of your heart that remains not converted? What do you intend to do?

7. What do the words, "Yahweh is God", mean for your own life?

Respond

These questions hopefully will lead your heart to prayer. What thoughts arise in your mind? What do you want to say to God? It is not necessary that you use holy words because you can in fact say anything to God. Perhaps you can pray for the Church, or for your country or for the problems of the world. Perhaps the thoughts that arise within you are of a more personal nature and you want to pray for your family or friends or for yourself. Do you want to have a more intimate relationship with the Lord?

Perhaps the following hymn from the book of the *Apocalypse* or *Revelation* (15:3-4) will help you in your conversations with God.

How great and wonderful are all your works, Lord God Almighty; upright and true are all your ways, King of nations. Who does not revere and glorify your name, O Lord? For you alone are holy, and all nations will come and adore you for the many acts of saving justice you have shown.

Rest

Normally we arrive at a point when our words or thoughts cannot express what is in our heart. Certainly vocal prayer will always be an important part of our relationship with God but perhaps there will also be an attraction to more silence. When we feel this attraction to silence, it can seem that we are wasting time. There will be a temptation to return to a form of prayer where we were in control and when at least we had the sensation of doing something, that is, a feeling that we were in fact praying. However, silence is a perfectly normal development of prayer. There is a time when we must leave aside our own words because they can no longer express what is in our heart. In the silence, God can listen to our heart, and in the silence we can listen to the gentle voice of God.

Contemplation occurs when we are captured and held in the hand of God. We experience the greatness of God and not only of the divine message. The encounter with God and the experience of God's nearness satisfy the desires of our heart. We are simply invited to rest in God and to have a simple and loving awareness of God's presence. The more we rest in God, the more profound will the divine work within us be. Gradually God shapes us to become what we were destined to be – images of the Son of God. At this point reading the Sacred Scripture becomes food for life and not just food for thought.

In the book of *Genesis,* Jacob had a dream and saw angels of God ascending and descending a ladder (*Genesis* 28:10-19). *Lectio Divina* is a little like this ladder. We are ascending and descending constantly even in one period of prayer. We do not remain in contemplation. We read the Word of God and meditate on it to prepare the way for prayer in the sense of opening our heart to God and this in turn prepares us for contemplation – resting in God. The first two stages can be present throughout the whole day, as we can read the Scriptures at different times and think about what we have read. When we come to the moment of prayer, understood here as a personal encounter with God, we can pray without the need for any lengthy preparation. Prayer in this sense prepares the way for contemplation.

To pray means to enter into a personal relationship with God. The work of God is to bring us to our full realisation, which means that we show forth the image of Christ that is planted deep within us. However, we cover over the true self – made in the image and likeness of God – with a shell. We have a number of masks with which we present ourselves to the world. Gradually we must allow God to very gently remove these masks one by one so that we can really be ourselves. God knows us but we do not know ourselves. Prayer is an encounter with God but it is also an encounter with ourselves.

At the beginning of any personal relationship silence is difficult but when we have reached a mature level silence can become a much more eloquent way of communicating. If silence is not just empty for you but full of meaning, I suggest that you leave aside your words and thoughts and just be with God in silence for a few minutes. Words and thoughts are good and useful but they remain "ours" in the sense that we are in control of the conversation. In the silence, we enter into God's world and we must learn a new language: "The Father spoke one Word, that was his Son, and He repeats it always in an eternal silence; in silence must it always be heard by the soul.[24]

Now I invite you to enter into your inner room, close the door and simply be in silence and God who knows everything that happens in secret will reward you (cf. *Matthew* 6:6). One can pray in any place but your room is interior, which means to enter within yourself where God dwells and communicate with God in that secret place. See the first Appendix for a method that might help you remain in the silence. In this prayer it is important only to consent to the presence and action of God in your life.

Act

How can you extend the interior silence to the rest of your life where there are so many distractions that threaten your peace? Listen to yourself. Be aware of your reactions in the ordinary events of life. How do you respond in situations where you feel that your self-assuredness or self-esteem is threatened (or the esteem that comes from others)? In a previous chapter, I mentioned the interior compact disk that always plays the same message, which is a commentary on everything that is happening from your own point of view. When we become more aware of this, we can learn to ignore it.

Saint Thérèse of Lisieux has suggested an ascetical practice that is much more effective than physical penances, that is, when someone says something that displeases you, do not respond immediately if it is not necessary for the sake of justice or the protection of another person. Also try to be aware of the feelings

24   St. John of the Cross, *Sayings of Light and Love*, 104.

that rise up in your heart. Let them come into awareness and offer them to God as if they were a very precious gift, instead of responding to the other person with a harsh word.[25]

Here are some possible words or phrases from the text of Scripture that we have been using. Perhaps you can carry one of these in your heart during the day:

"the word of Yahweh"

"Answer me, O Yahweh, answer me

"I am your servant"

"Yahweh's fire"

"Yahweh is God"

The people responded to the fire from God with an act of faith, "Yahweh is God! Yahweh is God!" Be aware of the presence of God with you today, and pray that God might rewrite your internal compact disk with the Good News of Jesus Christ.

---

25 Manuscript A, 68v.

The prophet Elijah's 'vision' of the Blessed Virgin Mary in a stained-glass window by G. P. Dagrant in the parish church of Lourdes, France.

Reflection 8
THE END OF THE DROUGHT
1 Kings **18:41-46**

Invocation

Oh God, you are the Creator and Lord of all. You have given to humanity the intelligence to understand many things and to build the earthly city. Help us to have faith in your providence and the wisdom to know that we have no lasting city here on earth. Send your Spirit that brooded over the waters at the beginning of creation, and help me to listen for your voice in all the events of the day. Through Christ our Lord. Amen.

Text

Read attentively the following text for the first time in order to understand the sense and to get hold of the basic facts of the story.

[41] Elijah said to Ahab, 'Go back now, eat and drink; for I hear the approaching sound of rain.' [42] While Ahab went back to eat and drink, Elijah climbed to the top of Carmel and bowed down to the ground, putting his face between his knees. [43] 'Now go up', he told his servant, 'and look out to sea.' He went up and looked. 'There is nothing at all,' he said. Seven times Elijah told him to go back. [44] The seventh time, the servant said, 'Now there is a cloud, small as a man's hand, rising from the sea.' Elijah said, 'Go and say to Ahab, "Harness the chariot and go down before the rain stops you." ' [45] And with that the sky grew dark with cloud and storm, and rain fell in torrents. Ahab mounted his chariot and made for Jezreel. [46] But the hand of Yahweh had come on Elijah and, hitching up his clothes, he ran ahead of Ahab all the way to Jezreel.

Read

Elijah announces the end of the drought as the final seal on the victory of Yahweh over Baal. He says to King Ahab to get up, eat and drink. This meal is a reminder of the covenant banquet that Moses, Aaron and the seventy elders celebrated on the mountain of God (*Exodus* 24:9-14). It seems that Ahab is still included as a member of the covenant community despite his sins.

Elijah prays while his servant looks out in the direction of the sea. Seven times (v.43) is a symbolic number to indicate "several times". The prophet is so convinced of the power of Yahweh that he can accept a long delay and that the sign of the small cloud is a guarantee of the rain. Before the rain, the sky becomes dark. This is very normal in Palestine during autumn and winter before a torrential rain.

Often people think that the fact that Elijah ran ahead of Ahab's chariot and horses is an example of the ecstatic power of the prophet. However, it would not be impossible for a human being to run faster than a horse and chariot all the way to Jezreel (about 25 kilometres), because a person could run directly while the horse and chariot would not be as fast on unstable ground. With the rain, the ground would be very difficult. Elijah wanted to return to Jezreel to whip up popular opinion against Jezebel. In the prophetic literature of the Bible "the hand of Yahweh" (v.46) is a habitual way to describe the irresistible divine action with regard to the human being (cf. *2 Kings* 3:15; *Ezekiel* 1:3, 3:22). He hitched up his clothes and ran. The prophet transforms himself into a humble servant of the king, perhaps to show that the king who has returned to faithfulness to God is worthy of honour.

The challenge for those who believe in God is to trust in this God and in no other, even when the alternative seems more relevant or popular.

Reflect

Read the text again to discover what it is that God wants to say to you. To help you in this meditation, here are some questions.

1. Do you trust God in the midst of the many difficulties of this world?

2. Can you discern the presence of God in the "signs of the times"?

3. God has great patience with you. Can you wait for God?

4. Do you want God to follow your will or are you ready to do God's will?

5. What does it mean for you to have hope in God?

Respond

In Carmelite spirituality, this text from the first *Book of Kings* has had a profound effect. At least from the end of the fourteenth century, in the Carmelite Order, a Marian meaning has been given to the sign of the small cloud. One Carmelite writer, Felip Ribot (†1391), wrote:

> *God revealed to Elijah that a female child, that is Blessed Mary, was prefigured in that little cloud. The littleness referred to her humility. She would be born from sinful human nature, symbolised by the sea. This child, from her birth, would be clean from every stain of sin, just like that little cloud emerging from the bitter sea, but itself free from all bitterness.*[26]

Certainly one cannot say that the true meaning of the text is what Felip Ribot wrote but it is an example of medieval thought. The Word of God can have various senses according to our receptivity. Our Lady was open to the Word and to the will of God. Mary is the first disciple of the Lord and is the model for listening to the Word. She did not only listen to the Word but also put it into practice (*Luke* 11:28). Mary can help us to pray. She took all the events of her life into her heart (*Luke* 2:51). We can learn from her how to respond to the Word of God. Along with Mary, sing to the Lord her song of joy, the *Magnificat* (*Luke* 1:46-55):

> [46] And Mary said: My soul proclaims the greatness of the Lord [47] and my spirit rejoices in God my Saviour; [48] because he has looked upon the humiliation of his servant. Yes, from now onwards all generations will call me blessed, [49] for the Almighty has done great things for me. Holy is his name, [50] and his faithful love extends age after age to those who fear him. [51] He has used the power of his arm, he has routed the arrogant of heart. [52] He has pulled down princes from their thrones and raised high the lowly. [53] He has filled the starving with good things, sent the rich away empty. [54] He has come to the help of Israel his servant, mindful of his faithful love [55] – according to the promise he made to our ancestors – of his mercy to Abraham and to his descendants for ever.

---

26 Emmanuele Boaga, *The Lady of the Place*, (Rome: Edizioni Carmelitane, 2001), pp. 50-51. See also Richard Copsey (ed.), *The Ten Books on the Way of Life and Great Deeds of the Carmelites*, (Faversham & Rome: Saint Albert's Press & Edizioni Carmelitane, 2005), p. 82.

Rest

A central concept for the spiritual journey is the personal relationship with God. The biblical writers used many metaphors to describe the human/divine relationship and the closest human reality was that of marriage. In order to grow in our relationship with God it is worthwhile trying to learn something from the normal development of a human relationship. I think that the spiritual process in marriage and in the consecrated life is the same, except that the means to arrive at the goal differ. Human life is a school of love; if we do not learn to love even if we have accomplished great things in the eyes of the world, we are like a sounding gong or a clashing cymbal (*1 Corinthians* 13:1). From the number of marriages that end in divorce, we can understand that learning to love is not at all easy.

Prayer is the gateway through which we enter into the relationship with God and the way to keep the flame alive in the relationship. Prayer is communication with God. A married couple cannot grow in their love without a continual communication; the rules that regulate human relationships can also be applied to the relationship with God. The temptation regarding prayer is to see it as a duty to be fulfilled rather than a way to communicate with God. If it were merely a duty, it would be quite simple. It would be enough to say the right words or fill the required time. Prayer is something else altogether. It must change us; if no change occurs, something is not quite right with our prayer or our life.

The goal of the spiritual journey is quite simply to become like God, to be able to see creation as God sees it and to love it as God loves it. The particular vocations (family, consecrated life, etc.) are different ways to arrive at the same goals. Every road must be a way to learn to love as God loves.

The human relationship, taken as a model for the development of our relationship with God, naturally has its limits. Christ is much more than a friend. He is the only one who can heal us and transform us totally, leading us to our fulfilment. In a normal human relationship, if one party decides not to continue a friendship, there is nothing more to be said or done. God, however, continually pursues us because only God knows what is our ultimate good.

God seeks us and invites us to enter more profoundly into the mystery of the life of the Trinity. It is only in God that we can find the answer to our own mystery. Prayer begins with the invitation that God presents to us in different ways. God is always very resourceful. God comes to us where we are, and we can be in a good place or not. God calls us from that place and invites us to begin a journey in the divine company. If we refuse, God continually repeats the invitation in different ways. God never gives up on any of us. When we do respond positively, God guides us delicately. Every relationship is different but we can learn something from the experience of others.

Prayer is a relationship with God. We are called to become intimate friends of God, in and through Jesus Christ. It is not easy to give permission to another person to enter our lives and to give to that person the freedom to wander the corridors of our heart, but a deep friendship demands this. Jesus Christ desires to transform us. The process of transformation is long and often arduous. God never gives up on us, but we must do our part so that the great work of transformation is brought to fulfilment.

In Carmelite spirituality, Mary, as well as being Mother, is also esteemed as Sister. She helps us, nourishes us and accompanies us on our journey through life. Her role is above all to help us enter and grow in our relationship with God. We must not only admire her privileges. These, in some way, point us towards our own future. Mary can help us more easily if we are open to her presence in our lives.

Act

Prayer is not only something reserved for special times but also it must affect our whole day and our whole life. We must find ways to keep our relationship with God alive and allow it to influence all our other relationships and everything else we do.

Your own ongoing relationship with God may suggest different ways to continue the intimate dialogue with God throughout the day but I suggest also some words or phrases from the text on which we have been meditating that you could carry in your heart and that could accompany you:

"Elijah climbed to the top of Carmel"

"bowed down to the ground"

"Now there is a cloud"

"the hand of Yahweh"

The prophet Elijah showed a great faith in the Lord when he said to Ahab that the rain was about to come after a long drought. We have said that in Carmelite spirituality the little cloud was connected with Our Lady. She is the first disciple of her Son and the model of faith for all Christians. In the Carmelite tradition, Mary and the prophet Elijah are the two biblical figures who inspire all Carmelites.[27] Try to spend today in company with Mary, your Mother and your Sister. She is a constant presence in your life, whether you appreciate it or not, and is always ready to help you in your every need. Carmelites wear a scapular to remind them of this constant presence and of our duty to imitate Mary's virtues.[28] All the various prayers to Our Lady can help you remain in the presence of God because you cannot think of her without thinking of God.

---

27 See Wilfrid McGreal, *At the Fountain of Elijah*, pp. 114-122; Peter Slattery, *The Springs of Carmel*, pp. 35-63.
28 See Joseph Chalmers, *Mary the Contemplative*, pp. 12-18.

Elijah encouraged by an angel. Window by Marc Chagall in the Stefanskirche, Mainz.

Reflection 9
ELIJAH ON THE WAY TO MOUNT HOREB
1 Kings **19:1-8**

Invocation

O Lord, save us from the perils of life. Help us when we think that our problems are greater than we can cope with, and when we do not want to carry on. Give us the bread of life so that we might continue our journey towards you. Amen.

Text

Read attentively the following text for the first time in order to capture the sense and to become aware of the basic facts of the story.

[1] When Ahab told Jezebel everything that Elijah had done, and how he had put all the prophets to the sword, [2] Jezebel sent a messenger to Elijah to say, 'May the gods bring unnameable ills on me and worse ills too, if by this time tomorrow I have not made your life like one of theirs!' [3] He was afraid and fled for his life. He came to Beersheba, a town of Judah, where he left his servant. [4] He himself went on into the desert, a day's journey, and sitting under a furze bush wished he were dead. 'Yahweh,' he said, 'I have had enough. Take my life; I am no better than my ancestors.' [5] Then he lay down and went to sleep. Then all of a sudden an angel touched him and said, 'Get up and eat.' [6] He looked round, and there at his head was a scone baked on hot stones, and a jar of water. He ate and drank and then lay down again. [7] But the angel of Yahweh came back a second time and touched him and said, 'Get up and eat, or the journey will be too long for you.' [8] So he got up and ate and drank, and strengthened by that food he walked for forty days and forty nights until he reached Horeb, God's mountain.

Read

After the tremendous victory on Mount Carmel, Elijah has to flee from the wrath of Jezebel who wants to kill him (v.1-3). Elijah went alone into the desert and he wished he were dead (v.4). He felt completely alone and he had no more strength to continue the fight against the idol worshipping. However, God does not let him fall into self-pity. Elijah has more work to do and God sends an angel to encourage the prophet. He must eat and drink in order to have sufficient strength for the journey to Mount Horeb (v.5-8).

The journey of Elijah to Horeb and the manifestation of God on the mountain are intimately connected with the tradition of Moses on Mount Sinai. Horeb and Sinai are two names for the same place. Elijah follows the same road that Moses took in order to receive a word of confirmation for his activity. Moses and Elijah appear together on the mountain of Transfiguration. Due to their courage and the numerous sufferings they had to endure in carrying out their prophetic mission, they were very suitable to stand beside Jesus, and to talk with him about his suffering that he had to undergo in Jerusalem (cf. *Luke* 9:31).

The words "hot stones" on which the scone was baked (v.6) are very rare in the Bible; in fact they occur only one other time, in *Isaiah* 6:6, when the seraphim take the hot stones from the altar in the Temple and touch the lips of the prophet Isaiah as a response to his expression of unworthiness to accept the task from the Lord. The angel of the Lord appears twice to Elijah. The first time, the mysterious figure is named simply "angel", which means messenger. The same word is used to describe the person sent by Jezebel to tell Elijah that she was looking to kill him. The listeners to this story would not know whether this messenger would bring the death that Elijah had requested or salvation. When the messenger is mentioned for a second time, the situation becomes clear: it is the messenger of the Lord. Then Elijah gets up and walks for forty days and forty nights towards Horeb, which is another name for Sinai, the sacred place where God gave the commandments to Moses. It is not necessary to believe that Elijah walked for exactly forty days because this number is symbolic and has a special significance in the Bible, being a reminder of the forty years that the chosen people spent in the desert before entering the Promised Land.

Reflect

Read the text once again in order to listen to what God is saying to you through this story.

To assist you to enter into this text and to receive some fruit from it, I have suggested some questions that you might like to think about:

1. What makes you afraid?

2. What do you do when someone or something interrupts your plans?

3. What can faith say to someone in the midst of depression?

4. Have you ever met a messenger from God?

5. At what point are you on your journey towards God?

Respond

Open your heart to God and say what is in your heart. Perhaps you want to talk about your fears for the future, or of your hopes, and pray for the courage to accept God's will even when this is contrary to what you want. Perhaps you want to ask for the strength to live faithfully the message of Christ. Perhaps you desire only to be in silence with your God. You can find a method to help you in the first Appendix. Or maybe the words of the psalmist (*Psalm* 13:1-6) can help you:

> [1] How long, Yahweh, will you forget me? For ever? How long will you turn away your face from me? [2] How long must I nurse rebellion in my soul, sorrow in my heart day and night? How long is the enemy to domineer over me? [3] Look down, answer me, Yahweh my God! Give light to my eyes or I shall fall into the sleep of death. [4] Or my foe will boast, 'I have overpowered him,' and my enemy have the joy of seeing me stumble. [5] As for me, I trust in your faithful love, Yahweh. Let my heart delight in your saving help, let me sing to Yahweh for his generosity to me, let me sing to the name of Yahweh the Most High!

Rest

Often we do not have a sense of the presence of God, even if our faith assures us that God is not really absent. We must walk in darkness and every now and then we feel a little more strength. In those times, God sends us an angel to give us what is necessary to continue our journey toward the Reign of God. However, it is not always easy to recognise an angel when one cannot see his or her wings! The angels who are sent to us are those people we meet throughout the day. We are too busy and too preoccupied and so we often fail to grasp what God is saying to us by means of some humble messenger. There is too much noise outside and inside us. The goal of contemplation is to bring to silence all this noise and so permit us to see the world the way God sees it and to love it with a divine love.

Life is not easy and at times it is difficult to discern the presence of God. We live in the midst of so much noise and often we are not aware of the voice of God. We need a little bit of silence in our lives in order to become aware of God in the midst of so many other voices.

Silence is not easy for us as we are surrounded by constant noise and we ourselves are filled with commentaries about ourselves and about other people. To find some silence in our lives, it is useful to discover a method that can help us remain in silence. The *prayer in secret* suggested in the first Appendix may be useful. Do not judge your prayer. Simply wait in the silence for God and when you become aware that you are thinking of something else, return ever so gently to the Lord by means of the sacred word that you have chosen, the word that represents for you everything you want to say to God. The sacred word is the symbol of your consent to the presence and purifying and transforming action of God in your life.

Act

In order to help you remain in the presence of God throughout the day, I suggest some words or phrases that you can carry in your heart as you go about your business. These are taken from the text itself.

"He was afraid"

"he fled for his life"

"he went into the desert"

"he wished he were dead"

"I have had enough"

"take my life"

"an angel touched him"

"Get up and eat"

"hot stones"

"The angel of Yahweh came back"

"strengthened by that food"

"God's mountain"

According to the text of the Bible that has come down to us, this scene of the flight of Elijah into the desert follows almost immediately on his great triumph on Mount Carmel. At the first threat from Queen Jezebel, the prophet Elijah goes into the desert and his trust in God just vanishes. He wants to die and only the intervention of the angel gives him the strength to continue his journey toward Mount Horeb, the mountain of God.

Today, try to be attentive to everything that happens and to the people you meet. Is God communicating with you in some small event of your day or through some person? Possibly the vehicle for God's message will be something that happens everyday or a person whom you know very well or someone you just happen to pass on the street. Keep your eyes and ears open today!

The prophet Elijah bearing his name (Elias) on a scroll.
Window at St. Edward the Confessor Church, Dringhouses, York.

Reflection 10
THE MEETING WITH GOD
1 Kings **19:9-18**

Invocation

O God, you are much greater than anything we can hope for and you go far beyond anything we can imagine. Teach us to be open to your coming in the way and at the time you choose. Teach us to perceive your voice in the sound of silence so that we can accomplish your will in all things. Amen.

Text

Read attentively the following text for the first time in order to capture the sense, and to gather the basic facts of the story.

9 There he went into a cave and spent the night there. Then the word of Yahweh came to him saying, 'What are you doing here, Elijah?' 10 He replied, 'I am full of jealous zeal for Yahweh Sabaoth, because the Israelites have abandoned your covenant, have torn down your altars and put your prophets to the sword. I am the only one left, and now they want to kill me.' 11 Then he was told, 'Go out and stand on the mountain before Yahweh.' For at that moment Yahweh was going by. A mighty hurricane split the mountains and shattered the rocks before Yahweh. But Yahweh was not in the hurricane. And after the hurricane, an earthquake. But Yahweh was not in the earthquake. 12 And after the earthquake, fire. But Yahweh was not in the fire. And after the fire, a light murmuring sound. 13 And when Elijah heard this, he covered his face with his cloak and went out and stood at the entrance of the cave. Then a voice came to him, which said, 'What are you doing here, Elijah?' 14 He replied, 'I am full of jealous zeal for Yahweh, God Sabaoth, because the Israelites have abandoned your covenant, have torn down your altars and put your prophets to the sword. I am the only one left and now they want to kill me.' 15 'Go,' Yahweh said, 'go back by the same way to the desert of Damascus. You must go

and anoint Hazael as king of Aram. [16] You must anoint Jehu son of Nimshi as king of Israel, and anoint Elisha son of Shaphat, of Abel-Meholah, as prophet to succeed you. [17] Anyone who escapes the sword of Hazael will be put to death by Jehu; and anyone who escapes the sword of Jehu will be put to death by Elisha. [18] But I shall spare seven thousand in Israel; all the knees that have not bent before Baal, all the mouths that have not kissed him.'

Read

The idea of the Old Testament is that prophet is the man of God, a title given many times to Elijah. The prophet Elijah is presented as a second Moses, especially on the journey to Horeb and in the meeting with God that took place there. Horeb is another name for Mount Sinai (*Exodus* 3:1). Moreover, the Bible presents Elijah as a man who spoke frequently and in an intimate way with God. Elijah returns to Horeb, the place where the revelation to Moses originally took place, and there it takes on a new vigour at the moment when the prophet despairs of the final destiny of this revelation. There are clearly two parallel stories here: *1 Kings* 19:9b-13a and 19:13b-19a.

From God's question, "What are you doing here, Elijah?" it seems that Elijah should not be on Mount Carmel but in Israel where the battle continues between Yahweh and Baal. Immediately Elijah gives a defensive answer, speaking of his personal zeal and the terrible religious situation in Israel. The Lord does not respond to Elijah's claims that he is filled with zeal. Elijah must get back to work. The Lord tells Elijah to remain on the mountain before the Lord. Probably the writer wants to evoke the tradition of Moses when the Lord passed before him (and perhaps even in this same cave – *Exodus* 33:19-23). The signs that typically introduced a visitation of God are not present in this scene. See *Exodus* 19:16-19 for example:

> [16] Now at daybreak two days later, there were peals of thunder and flashes of lightning, dense cloud on the mountain and a very loud trumpet blast; and, in the camp, all the people trembled. [17] Then Moses led the people out of the camp to meet God; and they took their stand at the bottom of the mountain. [18] Mount Sinai was entirely wrapped in smoke, because Yahweh had descended on it in the form of fire. The smoke rose like smoke from a furnace and the whole mountain shook violently. [19] Louder and louder grew the trumpeting. Moses spoke, and God answered him in the thunder."

See also *Judges* 5:4-5; *Psalm* 18:13, 68:9; *Nahum* 1:3-5; *Habakkuk* 3:4-6.

God is not in the storm or in the earthquake or in the fire. Probably there is an intentional contrast between Baal, the god of storms, and Yahweh (the Lord), whose sound is unique. After the fire, there is a great peace (literally, "the sound of a thin silence" or the sound of an absolute silence). Traditionally this silent sound has been translated "the sound of a gentle breeze" and in the text we are using, "a light murmuring sound". There is one other time in the Bible when the words "sound" and "silence" can be found together:

> It paused, but its likeness I could not discern; a figure was before
> my eyes, and I heard a still small voice. (*Job* 4:16)[29]

Probably this "small voice" or "light murmuring sound" means a very soft and low sound. This sound on Mount Horeb suggests that the actions of God are not always obvious but often one must discern the presence of God in the slow working-out of history. Elijah covered his face either out of respect (cf. *Exodus* 3:6) or because of the common belief that no one could see God and live to tell the tale (cf. *Judges* 13:22).

The gentle sound is not a romantic concept but throws all Elijah's ideas into confusion. God is not in the earthquake nor in the fire nor in the mighty wind. Yahweh is a God who cannot be controlled; God is always surprising. Also Elijah, the great prophet of God and the man of God, cannot grasp hold of God. Elijah must discern the presence of God and the divine action in the midst of silence. The victory on Mount Carmel with a bolt of lightning will no more be Yahweh's normal way of operating. The prophet Elijah must adjust his methods in order to follow what God wants. The gentle breeze, or the sheer silence, has broken the expectations of the past and has opened a new dimension for a new experience of God. Elijah discovers that God is present despite the fact that the traditional signs heralding God's presence are not in evidence.

Reflect

Read the text again in order to listen to the message that God has for you. I offer a few questions to help you work with the text.

---

29 This text is taken from the *New American Catholic Bible* (New Jersey: Thomas Nelson Inc., 1971). *The New Jerusalem Bible*, which we are using in this book, does not seem to be entirely accurate on this particular text.

1. In the text God asked, "What are you doing here, Elijah?" What would your answer be if the same question were posed to you in your own situation?

2. What do you expect from God and what is your favourite image of God?

3. Elijah became aware of the presence of God "in the light murmuring sound". Where can you meet God today? Have you ever been surprised by the presence of God in situations where you never thought of encountering God?

4. Elijah felt himself alone but God told him that there were seven thousand others who had not bent the knee to Baal. Are you sufficiently aware of other Christians in your own spiritual life?

Respond

What would you like to say to God now? What do you feel within yourself when God does not act according to your plans? Are you ready for the revelation of God at any moment and in an unusual way? Elijah met God but not in the way he expected and Elijah had to change. God is always with us but we are not always with God. Open your heart to God now. Perhaps the following psalm (139:1-18) could help you:

[1] Yahweh, you examine me and know me, [2] you know when I sit, when I rise, you understand my thoughts from afar. [3] You watch when I walk or lie down, you know every detail of my conduct. [4] A word is not yet on my tongue before you, Yahweh, know all about it. [5] You fence me in, behind and in front, you have laid your hand upon me. [6] Such amazing knowledge is beyond me, a height to which I cannot attain. [7] Where shall I go to escape your spirit? Where shall I flee from your presence? [8] If I scale the heavens you are there, if I lie flat in Sheol, there you are. [9] If I speed away on the wings of the dawn, if I dwell beyond the ocean, [10] even there your hand will be guiding me, your right hand holding me fast. [11] I will say, 'Let the darkness cover me, and the night wrap itself around me,' [12] even darkness to you is not dark, and night is as clear as the day. [13] You created my inmost self, knit me together in my mother's womb. [14] For so many marvels I thank you; a wonder am I, and all your works are wonders. You knew me through and through, [15]

my being held no secrets from you, when I was being formed in secret, textured in the depths of the earth. [16] Your eyes could see my embryo. In your book all my days were inscribed, every one that was fixed is there. [17] How hard for me to grasp your thoughts, how many, God, there are! [18] If I count them, they are more than the grains of sand; if I come to an end, I am still with you.

Rest

The meeting between God and Elijah on Mount Horeb in the sound of a gentle breeze or in the sound of sheer silence or in the light murmuring sound has been much used for prayer and meditation over the centuries. We have seen that this experience must have been very difficult for the prophet Elijah because God came to meet him in a totally unexpected way. God did not come in the earthquake or in the fire or in the mighty wind, all the ways that God had used previously to announce the divine presence, but instead God came in silence.

Through the gift of faith we can know something about God but God always goes beyond our human concepts. The contemplative way leads to the complete transformation of the human person whereby our human ways of seeing, loving and interacting with the world, which are always limited, become divine ways. This is naturally the work of God but we must do everything in our power to facilitate and accept this personal and structural transformation. We must learn gradually who is God. An intellectual knowledge of the fundamental truths of the faith is important. However, it is one thing to intellectually grasp what love means, and another thing to know love by experience. The experience of God helps us to grasp theological concepts in a new way. Often God will surprise us and act completely outside our limited possibilities. Little by little we have to learn to see everything from another perspective. Everything may remain the same but may in fact appear totally different because we have a different way of seeing.

Prayer is in some way relating to God, and so every prayer is good, and every method of prayer that helps us to grow in our relationship with God can be helpful. Just as in a human relationship, so also in the relationship with God, it is very normal for it to become simpler with the passage of time. We become less and less surprised when God approaches us in a way that we are not used to. We learn to accept that we are always at the beginning of the spiritual journey and that God is always ahead of us.

All prayer, if it is authentic, must be open to contemplation in the sense that it must encourage the transformation of the human heart. The Christian tradition gives various suggestions regarding methods of prayer that have proved their worth over the centuries. After the liturgy, which is the prayer of the whole Body of Christ, head and members, comes *Lectio Divina*, the prayerful reading of the Word of God. Then we have many devotions approved by the Church. All these devotions or methods of prayer must be directed toward the contemplation of God and our own transformation.

Every personal relationship with God is unique and must be expressed in a unique way. Each individual must find suitable ways to keep alive his or her relationship with God. The *prayer of silence* (or prayer in secret) is a modern method, based on the ancient Christian tradition. It is a method to assist the movement from the third phase of *Lectio Divina* (praying or responding) to the fourth (contemplating, resting). Many people have found a great help for their own spiritual journey in this method.

I suggest now that you leave this book aside and enter into dialogue with God, using any method that helps you to remain in the presence of God. The important thing is not the method, but whether your heart is open to God and ready to be surprised by God who will come to you in ways that you cannot foresee.

Act

To help the process of allowing the Word of God to take deep root in you, I here suggest some phrases or words that could be used as a reminder of God's presence in the midst of a busy day:

"he went into the cave"

"the Word of Yahweh"

"what are you doing here?"

"I am full of zeal"

"your covenant"

"I am the only one left"

"before Yahweh"

"the Lord was not in the hurricane"

"a light murmuring sound"

"he covered his face"

Prayer is the way we can enter into a relationship with God and so it has many expressions. Prayer should reflect life, which means that our life must be in tune with what we profess. Being human beings, sin is always a possibility for us. It is important to use the normal remedies for sin that the Church offers.

Any experience of God is only important if it leads us to living more in conformity with the message of Jesus. The prophet Elijah received a new mission after his experience of God on the mountain. Each one of us has a particular mission; we are unique individuals and we alone can fulfil our unique mission. This mission may seem very humble or it may seem very important, but really everything is important for God. Our mission will be in conformity with our basic vocation as a married person, a parent, a member of a religious congregation, priest, etc. When the angel announced to Mary that her mission was to be the Mother of the Saviour, she accepted with simplicity and humility:

> Mary said, 'You see before you the Lord's servant, let it happen to me as you have said.' (*Luke* 1:38).

What is your mission today? Ask Mary, the Mother of Jesus to help you in discovering and accepting with humility what God wants of you.

*A window depicting the prophet Elisha by Richard Joseph King
in the National Shrine of Saint Jude, Faversham, Kent.*

Reflection 11
<u>VOCATION OF ELISHA</u>
1 Kings **19:19-21**

<u>Invocation</u>

Lord, you have called us to follow you in some way. Give us the grace to respond generously to your Word in order to accomplish your will in our lives and in our world. Through Christ our Lord. Amen.

<u>Text</u>

Read attentively the following text for the first time in order to capture the sense and to grasp the basic facts of the story.

> [19] Leaving there, he came on Elisha son of Shaphat as he was ploughing behind twelve yoke of oxen, he himself being with the twelfth. Elijah passed near to him and threw his cloak over him. [20] Elisha left his oxen and ran after Elijah. 'Let me kiss my father and mother, then I will follow you,' he said. Elijah answered, 'Go, go back; for have I done anything to you?' [21] Elisha turned away, took a yoke of oxen and slaughtered them. He used the oxen's tackle for cooking the meat, which he gave the people to eat. He then rose and, following Elijah, became his servant.

<u>Read</u>

The first thing that Elijah must do according to *1 Kings* 19:15-16 is to nominate Elisha as his successor. Elijah throws his mantle over Elisha, and with this gesture, he transfers to Elisha his spirit and his mission. Elisha appears as a rich farmer. Elijah is a prophet who travels around constantly. Acceptance of Elijah's action means that Elisha must leave behind his family and his property. In the text there is an emphasis on the absolute nature of the call. One can see the same kind of call in the New Testament, for example in *Matthew* 8:21 and *Luke* 9:61. It seems that Elisha will accept this mission but with certain conditions. The response of Elijah can be understood in two ways: it could be a complete refusal or a warning. Elijah will not accept conditions. It is not clear whether

Elisha says goodbye to his parents, but he leaves his property behind with great determination and gives it away. From now on, Elisha is the servant of Elijah and he follows him.

Reflect

Read the text of *1 Kings* 19:19-21 again in order to listen to what God wants from you. To help you get into this text, here are some questions to reflect on. They may help you respond to what God is saying to you.

1. What is your experience of God's call?

2. Elisha wanted to embrace his parents before following Elijah. What is (or was) your relationship with your parents and what can you learn from this for your relationship to God?

3. What did you learn about God from your parents?

4. Elisha abandoned his oxen. Have you abandoned anything in order to follow Christ?

5. What is your relationship with Christ now?

Respond

Becoming a disciple can be costly (for examples see *Luke* 9:57-62; *Matthew* 8:18-22, 19:23-30; *Mark* 10:23-31). God wants our complete salvation. God sent the only Son to show us the way to eternal life and to show us how to live a truly human life. Jesus Christ did not promise an easy life for his followers; on the contrary, he invited us to accompany him to Calvary, carrying the cross with him so that we would receive new life from God. We cannot imagine what has been prepared for those who love God. Let us pray for the grace to accept the will of God and to be faithful to the Gospel in the midst of the ups and downs of life.

> Father,
> I abandon myself into your hands,
> do with me what you will.
> Whatever you may do I thank you:
> I am ready for all, I accept all.
> Let only your will be done in me
> and in all your creatures.

I wish no more than this, O Lord.
Into your hands I commend my soul;
I offer it to you
with all the love of my heart
for I love you, Lord,
and so need to give myself,
to surrender myself
into your hands
without reserve
and with boundless confidence
for you are my Father.[30]

Rest

The process of transformation normally takes a long time because it brings about a radical change in the human being. Transformation is not only a change that helps one live a good Christian life. Through this spiritual process the human ways of thinking, loving and behaving are transformed into divine ways. The journey of transformation is normally long because the purification and change that take place are so profound. It is not a case of simply changing ideas or opinions. It is a fundamental transformation of the way we relate to the world around us, to other people and to God. The process of Christian transformation leads the individual to a profound change of perspective: from an all too human way of seeing things to God's way.

A classic concept of Christian spirituality is the *dark night*, which is amply explained in the writings of Saint John of the Cross.[31] The dark night is an experience that can go on for many years, of the experience of God coming closer. However, the light of God is so brilliant that we are blinded and can see nothing. It can seem that God is very far away but in fact is very near. The experience of the dark night can be difficult because we feel our weakness and the fact that we are sinners in need of the mercy of God.

The dark night brings us to the awareness of who we are and just how much we are attached to our own ideas of what is happiness and how to arrive at it. This is a very important part of the process of transformation because it helps us to realise how these ideas for happiness lead instead to misery. There is darkness because we have not let go of our ideas to attain happiness, and we have not received as

---

30 Prayer of Blessed Charles de Foucauld taken from a prayer card.
31 The whole of the books *The Ascent of Mount Carmel* and *The Dark Night* are about this concept.

yet the fullness of true joy that comes only from the Lord. This is an invitation to wait in the darkness for God who is always faithful. One can experience the dark night in many ways but often, at the beginning, a vague sense of dissatisfaction with the whole of life is felt. When one falls in love, at the beginning, life with the beloved promises to bring complete happiness. However, only God suffices for the human heart and no human being has the capacity to fulfil us totally. The author Kahlil Gibran has written the following about marriage:

> Give your hearts, but not into each other's keeping.
> For only the hand of Life can contain your hearts.
> And stand together yet not too near together:
> For the pillars, of the Temple stand apart
> And the oak tree and the cypress grow not in each other's shadow.[32]

The honeymoon does not last long. Life can be difficult and often we cannot understand why many things happen. However, God is in the middle of all our personal relationships and uses every event, small or great, for our spiritual growth. If we are really seeking the will of God, all the difficulties of life form part of the dark night experience, which is not a punishment, but a sign of God's love for us, and a guarantee that the Lord is setting us free to really be ourselves. The dark night is an essential part of our journey toward our complete liberation.

In the dark night we lose control and we must let ourselves be led by God. There comes a time in prayer when all our beautiful words no longer satisfy and we are led into silence. In the first Appendix there is a suggested method of prayer to help you remain in the silence, waiting for God to purify and transform you.

Act

How can we bring our relationship with God into daily life and live faithfully our following of Christ? There follows some phrases from the text that might help us to remember the presence of God throughout the day:

"he threw his cloak over him"

"he ran after Elijah"

"I will follow you"

"he became his servant"

---

32 Kahlil Gibran, *The Prophet*, (William Heinemann Ltd., 1926 & 1980), p. 19.

Elisha left all and followed Elijah. Jesus Christ calls some people to leave everything and follow him in order to dedicate their whole lives to the building of the Reign of God. Other people are called to transform this world by means of a Christian marriage, a job, suffering, etc. Each of us has a vocation and we have also received the grace to live it faithfully.

Are you faithful to your vocation? Pray for the grace to continue to be faithful, or to be faithful once again, and to listen to the voice of God in all the events, big or small, of the day.

*Elisha depicted in a medieval stained glass 'Tree of Jesse' window
in the Church of Saint Mary in Shrewsbury.*

Reflection 12
NABOTH'S VINEYARD
1 Kings **21:1-18**

Invocation

O God, we live in a world of injustice. Help me to live always according to your Word so that I can work with you for the transformation of this world. Help me now to listen to your Word that it may transform my whole existence. Through Christ our Lord. Amen.

Text

Read attentively the following text for the first time in order to capture the sense and grasp the basic facts of the story.

¹ Naboth of Jezreel had a vineyard close by the palace of Ahab king of Samaria, ² and Ahab said to Naboth, 'Give me your vineyard to be my vegetable garden, since it adjoins my palace; I will give you a better vineyard for it or, if you prefer, I will give you its value in money.' ³ Naboth, however, said to Ahab, 'Yahweh forbid that I should give you my ancestral heritage!' ⁴ Ahab went home gloomy and out of temper at the words of Naboth of Jezreel, 'I will not give you my heritage from my ancestors.' He lay down on his bed and turned his face away and refused to eat. ⁵ His wife Jezebel came to him. 'Why are you so dispirited,' she said, 'that you refuse to eat?' ⁶ He said, 'I have been talking to Naboth of Jezreel. I said, "Give me your vineyard either for money or, if you prefer, for another vineyard in exchange." But he said, "I will not give you my vineyard." ' ⁷ Then his wife Jezebel said, 'Some king of Israel you make! Get up, eat and take heart; I myself shall get you the vineyard of Naboth the Jezreelite.' ⁸ So she wrote a letter in Ahab's name and sealed it with his seal, sending the letter to the elders and notables of the city where Naboth lived. ⁹ In the letter, she wrote, 'Proclaim a fast, and put Naboth in a prominent place among the people. ¹⁰ There confront him with a couple of scoundrels who will accuse him as follows, "You have cursed God and the king." Then

take him outside and stone him to death.' [11] The men of Naboth's city, the elders and notables living in his city, did what Jezebel ordered, as was written in the letter which she had sent him. [12] They proclaimed a fast and put Naboth in a prominent place among the people. [13] The two scoundrels then came and confronted him, and the scoundrels then publicly accused Naboth as follows, 'Naboth has cursed God and the king.' He was then taken outside the city and stoned to death. [14] They then sent word to Jezebel, 'Naboth has been stoned to death.' [15] When Jezebel heard that Naboth had been stoned to death, she said to Ahab, 'Get up! Take possession of the vineyard which Naboth of Jezreel refused to sell you, for Naboth is no longer alive, he is dead.' [16] When Ahab heard that Naboth was dead, he got up to go down to the vineyard of Naboth of Jezreel and take possession of it. [17] Then the word of Yahweh came to Elijah the Tishbite, [18] 'Up! Go down to meet Ahab king of Israel, in Samaria. You will find him in Naboth's vineyard; he has gone down to take possession of it.'

Read

The account of Naboth is not similar to the other stories about Elijah because it does not concern Elijah directly but Naboth, Ahab and Jezebel. This episode was taken out of the cycle of Elijah stories and was placed between Ahab's two wars in order to connect the death of the king recounted at the end of chapter 22 of the first *Book of Kings*, with the oracle of God that announces it beforehand. Elijah defends justice most passionately and God manifests the depths of divine mercy toward sinners. The prophet appears only after the death of Naboth to announce the judgment of Yahweh.

The king, Ahab, wanted to buy Naboth's vineyard either by means of an exchange or for money (v.1-2). The request at first seems to be very reasonable but the answer of Naboth is notable: "Yahweh forbid that I should give you my ancestral heritage!" (v.3). The motive given by Naboth for his refusal to sell his vineyard is religious in nature. You can see the fundamental Israelite legislation in the book of *Leviticus* 25:23: 'The land shall not be sold so as to lose all rights over it, because the land is mine and you are residents and my guests.' Israel was the territory of Yahweh (*Joshua* 22:19). God conquered the land and gave it to the chosen people. Naboth believed that he held the land directly from God and no one, not even the king, had the right to take it from him.

The legal concept of property in Israel changed when the society moved from a loose federation of tribes to a centralised state under the monarchy. The king sought more and more land and other property in order to maintain the royal court and to pay the costs of government. Ahab understood that he could do nothing further in the face of Naboth's refusal. However, Jezebel had another point of view regarding property and royal authority. Immediately she began to plot to take over Naboth's vineyard (v.7). He is accused of blasphemy and is put to death according to the Law (*Leviticus* 24:14-16). Naboth is accused of cursing God, though the Hebrew text replaces the word "curse" with "bless" out of deference for the name of God. We read in *2 Kings* 9:26 that all the children of Naboth were also killed.

When Ahab was about to enter into possession of Naboth's vineyard, Elijah arrived with a condemnation from Yahweh. Elijah prophesised the fall of the house of Omri, the father of Ahab (v.20-24, 29) and this prophesy is fulfilled in *2 Kings* 9-10. Hearing the words of Elijah, Ahab repents and so does not see the end of his dynasty. However, this will take place after his death. (v.27-29).

Reflect

Read the text again to listen to what God wants to say to you. To help you interiorise what God wants to teach you by means of this text of Scripture, here are some questions for your reflection:

1. Have you ever suffered an injustice?

2. Did you experience God in some way through this experience?

3. Have you grown as a human being by means of your experience of life?

4. Have you forgiven those who did you wrong?

5. Ahab was very disappointed with Naboth's response and he acted like a spoiled child. What is your reaction when faced with the disappointments of life?

Respond

The powerful people in every age have found ways to cheat the poor. We can see in this story how sin grows in intensity – jealousy leads to bearing false witness which in turn leads to murder. Jealousy is put on the same level as idolatry. Pray for those who have done you wrong.

> Jesus said, 'Father, forgive them; they do not know what they are doing.' (*Luke* 23, 34).

> Father, may your name be held holy,your kingdom come;
> give us each day our daily bread,
> and forgive us our sins,
> for we ourselves forgive each one who is in debt to us.
> And do not put us to the test. (*Luke* 11:2-4).

Rest

One fruit that can be expected from a faithful commitment to some way of prayer that opens our heart to the presence and action of God, like the *prayer in secret* (see the first Appendix), is a gradual growth in unconditional love. We tend to restrict our love in various ways but the love of God is universal, and when we seek to rest in God we learn to love from the source of all love. As we let go of our own idea of who deserves our love, gradually we learn to see people as God sees them. We learn compassion and respect for the liberty of others. We set people free by our love and do not tie them up in an emotional web. We begin to find God in other people and also we find others in God. God loves each human being and when we rest in the source of all love, we learn to love as God loves.

When we are faithful to the daily encounter with God, the process of transformation intensifies in us. God wants to make us holy but often we impede the divine work because we are not quite ready to let go of our own ways. The prayer in secret teaches us to let go of our fear of the unknown and to entrust ourselves radically to God who alone can save us. This radical trust makes the process of transformation move more quickly. God heals the roots of our sin and the new self can come to birth.

Only God can satisfy every desire of the human heart. Alone, we cannot make our lives fruitful. This is the work of God who desires to transform us. Finally we will bear abundant fruit that will last. The fruit of the action of the Spirit in our lives is 'love, joy, peace, patience, kindness, goodness, trustfulness, gentleness and self-control' (*Galatians* 5:22-23). This is the fruit of the Holy Spirit and does not come from our own efforts. Of course we have to co-operate and we can do so by letting go of our emotional programmes for happiness and entrusting our lives to God, who will melt us, mould us, fill us and use us for the benefit of many people.

Enter into a period of silence, and give yourself some space to listen to God. Consent to the divine presence and purifying and transforming action.

Act

In our western societies we live in what has been called post-Christian and secularised times in which the message of the Gospel has been offered and rejected by many. We must be clear. Our societies have not necessarily rejected the Gospel or God; many people may have rejected the way in which the Gospel has sometimes been presented and a particular understanding of God. It is often said that there is a great interest in spirituality but little in institutional religion. Of course we are speaking rather generally because there is still much good going on within our Christian communities. There is clearly a need for a new evangelisation: we must find a new language to speak of Christ to modern people.

The most important thing for each of us is to live our faith. God loves everyone and we must treat each person as a child of God.

> [12] As the chosen of God, then, the holy people whom he loves, you are to be clothed in heartfelt compassion, in generosity and humility, gentleness and patience. [13] Bear with one another; forgive each other if one of you has a complaint against another. The Lord has forgiven you; now you must do the same. [14] Over all these clothes, put on love, the perfect bond. (*Colossians* 3:12-14).

Try to put these words into practice today.

The prophet Elijah depicted in the chapel of the
National Shrine of Saint Thérèse in Darien, Illinois, U.S.A.

Reflection 13
ILLNESS OF KING ACAZIAH
2 Kings **1:1-8**

Invocation

O Lord of life, help me to accept your will. If you give me health, let me work for your Kingdom. If you give me illness, let me offer it for your glory. Thank you for life. Help me not to damage either my own life or that of others by my actions. I ask this through Christ our Lord. Amen.

Text

Read attentively the following text for the first time in order to capture the sense and to grasp the basic facts of the story.

¹ After Ahab's death Moab rebelled against Israel. ² Ahaziah had fallen from the balcony of his upper room in Samaria, and was lying ill; so he sent messengers, saying to them, 'Go and consult Baal-Zebub god of Ekron and ask whether I shall recover from my illness.' ³ But the angel of Yahweh said to Elijah the Tishbite, 'Up! Go and intercept the king of Samaria's messengers. Say to them, "Is there no God in Israel, for you to go and consult Baal-Zebub god of Ekron? ⁴ Yahweh says this: You will never leave the bed you have got into; you are certainly going to die." ' And Elijah set out. ⁵ The messengers returned to the king, who said, 'Why have you come back?' ⁶ 'A man came to meet us,' they answered. 'He said, "Go back to the king who sent you and tell him: Yahweh says this: Is there no God in Israel, for you to go and consult Baal-Zebub god of Ekron? For this, you will never leave the bed you have got into; you are certainly going to die." ' ⁷ He said, 'This man who met you and said all this, what was he like?' ⁸ 'A man wearing a hair cloak', they answered, 'and a leather loincloth.' 'It was Elijah the Tishbite,' he said.

Read

Acaziah became king after the death of his father, Ahab. Acaziah fell and was very seriously injured. He sent messengers to Baalzebub, the god of Ekron (v.2) in order to find out whether he would recover or not (v.2). Baalzebub means "Baal the fly" or "Baal the plague", perhaps a deliberate distortion of the name "Baalzebul" – "Baal the Prince". See also in the New Testament *Matthew* 10:25 (also *Matthew* 12:24, 27; *Mark* 3:22; *Luke* 11:15, 18-19):

> It is enough for disciple to grow to be like teacher, and slave like master. If they have called the master of the house "Beelzebul", how much more the members of his household?

The fact that the king has sent for an oracle to an idol caused the anger of Yahweh, which Elijah expresses. Yahweh gives the answer to Acaziah's question: certainly you will die! (v.4).

Reflect

Read the text again in order to listen to what God wants to say to you. To assist your reflection on this text, here are some questions.

1. What has been your experience of illness?

2. Where was God in this experience?

3. Did you manage to pray while you were ill?

4. For what did you pray? Health? Acceptance?

5. What answer did you receive to your prayers?

6. Have you ever had to say something very difficult to someone?

Respond

All the stories in the *Books of the Kings* tell of the unfaithfulness of the kings to the covenant with God. The way we live will have some consequences. Let us pray that our lives may be in harmony with the Gospel.

> [14] This, then, is what I pray, kneeling before the Father, [15] from whom every fatherhood, in heaven or on earth, takes its name. [16] In the abundance of his glory may he, through his Spirit, enable you to grow firm in power with regard to your inner self, [17] so that Christ

may live in your hearts through faith, and then, planted in love and built on love, [18] with all God's holy people you will have the strength to grasp the breadth and the length, the height and the depth; [19] so that, knowing the love of Christ, which is beyond knowledge, you may be filled with the utter fullness of God. [20] Glory be to him whose power, working in us, can do infinitely more than we can ask or imagine; [21] glory be to him from generation to generation in the Church and in Christ Jesus for ever and ever. Amen. (*Ephesians* 3:14-21).

Rest

The movement of *Lectio Divina* is towards contemplation, which is the phase in which the friendship with Christ reaches maturity. The process of transformation in Christ goes on in every aspect of life but the phase of contemplation brings the process to a peak. In contemplation we reach union with God. This is not the end of the journey but a new beginning. Intimacy has many expressions and we will never come to the end of our exploration because only God can search the depths of God. (cf. *Romans* 11:33-36).

Contemplative prayer is qualitatively different from every other kind of prayer that may have preceded it. If we are given the grace of contemplative prayer, we have no more control. It is the transforming action of God in us; in a certain sense it is as if we are put to sleep, while God, the great healer, works within us at a profound level to transform the hidden recesses of our heart in the image of Christ. We are not of course completely passive, as it says in the *Song of Songs*: 'I sleep but my heart watches' (5:2). The process of contemplation develops throughout the whole of life, but it reaches a peak in contemplative prayer. One cannot grasp hold of contemplation; one can only receive.

The goal of the Christian life is that the will of God come to fruition in each person and in our world. In order that this may take place, we need to be transformed, as does the whole of creation, which waits with eager longing for the revelation of the children of God. As Saint Paul writes in his *Letter to the Romans* (8:18-23):

> [18] I think that what we suffer in this life can never be compared to the glory, as yet unrevealed, which is waiting for us. [19] The whole creation is eagerly waiting for God to reveal his children. [20] It was not for any fault on the part of creation that it was made unable to attain its purpose, it was made so by God; but creation still retains

the hope [21] of being freed, like us, from its slavery to decadence, to enjoy the same freedom and glory as the children of God. [22] From the beginning till now the entire creation, as we know, has been groaning in one great act of giving birth; [23] and not only creation, but all of us who possess the first-fruits of the Spirit, we too groan inwardly as we wait for our bodies to be set free.

The goal of the spiritual journey is to be transformed by God. It is a profound change in the way in which we think, behave and love. We leave behind our usual human ways, which of their nature are limited, in order to live according to God's way. Put more directly, the Christian vocation is to become like God. The early Fathers of the Church spoke and wrote a great deal about the divinisation of the human being.[33] Every aspect of human life must be transformed. This normally is a long and slow process, which rarely is completed during this life, according to human judgment, but perhaps God judges differently. To live a spiritual life, or to follow a spiritual journey, is to become involved in this process of transformation. Relating to other people aids this process of growth and transformation greatly because we learn so much about ourselves through our reactions to the ups and downs of life, if we have eyes to see and ears to hear.

Contemplation is a gift of God, as is the whole of the spiritual journey, which is the process toward the transformation of the human heart. The goal of this journey is to allow the Word to transform us, that is to say, to change the motivations of our heart so that we may act from a pure heart and begin to see everything from the divine perspective, or with the eyes of God. The transformed human heart can love in a divine way, which is a completely gratuitous love toward everyone.

Contemplation goes beyond the specific time we allot to prayer; it involves the whole of life. It involves us in a process of purification and transformation with the goal of uniting us with Christ. We can feel very far from that ideal but God takes us as we are. Looking back over our lives, we have arrived at this point through all sorts of highs and lows. We have all been badly treated and disappointed at times. We can choose how to respond to the experiences of life. We can respond in a spirit of faith or like those who live a practical atheism, without any reference to God. Responding with faith means accepting our experience of life, the bad as well as the good, and renewing our "yes" to the presence and action of God in our life. God does not necessarily send us

---

33 See also John Welch, *The Carmelite Way*, (New Jersey: Paulist Press, 1996), chapter 10.

the sufferings that we have had to face, but writes straight with crooked lines. God uses the circumstances of life to purify us and continue the sacred work of transformation within us. 'We know that everything works together for those who love God, those who were called according to the divine plan.' (*Romans* 8:28).

In the first Appendix I suggest a method of prayer that could help to open you to the call of God and to a deeper prayer life. It is only one method among many but perhaps it may help you.

ACT

Here are some phrases from the text we have been considering to remind you of the presence of God throughout the day:

"the angel of Yahweh"

"Yahweh says this"

"Elijah set out"

"is there no God in Israel?"

Perhaps you could repeat one of these phrases from time to time during the day.

Is there some sick person you should visit? Why not do it today to bring the sick person some comfort with your presence. Prayer must be lived in daily life and in the little things, not only at the major moments of our existence.

*A window depicting the prophet Elijah in St. Michael and All Angels Anglican
Church, Winnipeg, Canada. The rays of light on Elijah's head are an allusion
to the Transfiguration of Christ, who is depicted in an adjoining window.*

Reflection 14
<u>THE ATTEMPT TO CAPTURE ELIJAH</u>
2 Kings **1:9-15**

<u>Invocation</u>

O Lord, your prophet Elijah was a man of God and your protection was always with him. Your strength is stronger than human evil. Protect me from all sin and from every temptation to put my will in place of yours. Amen.

<u>Text</u>

Read attentively the following text for the first time in order to capture the sense and to grasp the basic facts of the story.

[9] He then sent a captain of fifty soldiers with his fifty men to Elijah, whom they found sitting on top of a hill; the captain went up to him and said, 'Man of God, the king says, "Come down."' [10] Elijah answered the captain, 'If I am a man of God, may fire fall from heaven and destroy both you and your fifty men.' And fire fell from heaven and destroyed him and his fifty men. [11] The king sent a second captain of fifty to him, again with fifty men, and he too went up and said, 'Man of God, this is the king's order, "Come down at once."' [12] Elijah answered them, 'If I am a man of God, may fire fall from heaven and destroy both you and your fifty men.' And lightning fell from heaven and destroyed him and his fifty men. [13] The king then sent a third captain of fifty to him, with another fifty men. The third captain of fifty came up to Elijah, fell on his knees before him and pleaded with him. 'Man of God,' he said, 'may my life and the lives of these fifty servants of yours count for something in your eyes. [14] Fire has fallen from heaven and destroyed two captains of fifties and their companies, but this time may my life count for something in your eyes!' [15] The angel of Yahweh said to Elijah, 'Go down with him; do not be afraid of him.' He rose and accompanied him down to the king.

Read

This passage stresses that the prophets of Yahweh were under divine protection and nothing, not even fifty soldiers, could harm them. Always the writer wants to teach that there is only one God – Yahweh.

The text might seem very strange to our eyes. Certainly it is not according to Jesus' teaching. There is a passage in the Gospels where Jesus was not welcomed in a Samaritan village and the disciples wanted to call fire from heaven to burn the whole village. Jesus reproved them.

> [51] Now it happened that as the time drew near for him to be taken up, he resolutely turned his face towards Jerusalem [52] and sent messengers ahead of him. These set out, and they went into a Samaritan village to make preparations for him, [53] but the people would not receive him because he was making for Jerusalem. [54] Seeing this, the disciples James and John said, 'Lord, do you want us to call down fire from heaven to burn them up?' [55] But he turned and rebuked them." (*Luke* 9:51-55).

Even though the disciples had shown that they did not understand the teaching of Jesus, at least they had a great faith in thinking that God would respond to their desire for vengeance! The disciples had to learn a great deal from Jesus. We too must be open to learning much.

We must remember that the revelation of God came through the vagaries of human history. The Word of God took flesh and became one of us. God is with us and is bringing our history to its fulfilment even though we may not understand how. The Old Testament finds its fulfilment in the New, and we must read the stories of the Old Testament in the light of the revelation brought to us by Jesus Christ.

Reflect

Read the text again in order to listen to what God wants to say to you. The story that we have been considering stresses the first commandment. The king believes that Baalzebub is the Lord of life, instead of God. Elijah, the man of God, displays the power of the true God and shows that idols are nothing. Here are some questions to assist your meditation:

1. Is there some idol in your life, that is to say something that takes God's place and by means of which you seek a lasting happiness – success, money, the good opinion of others, etc.?

2. What does happiness mean for you?

3. Have you ever experienced the power of God? What did it feel like?

4. Have you ever experienced the mercy of God? How did that change your outlook?

5. What can you learn from God's merciful love toward you?

Respond

Perhaps this text seems very strange to you in the sense that the idea of God is different from what we are used to in the Gospel. However we can read the Old Testament in the light of the Gospel. The Old Testament bears witness to the story of the relationship between God and humanity. Gradually the true nature of God is revealed in the events of history and especially in the history of the chosen people. The fullness of the revelation about God did not come until the life, death and resurrection of Jesus Christ.

It is always good to speak to God with one's own words but the Bible and the Christian tradition can also help. This hymn from the New Testament (*Philippians* 2:5-11) can throw light on the idea of God and of God's love for us:

> [5] Make your own the mind of Christ Jesus: [6] Who, being in the form of God, did not count equality with God something to be grasped. [7] But he emptied himself, taking the form of a slave, becoming as human beings are; and being in every way like a human being, [8] he was humbler yet, even to accepting death, death on a cross. [9] And for this God raised him high, and gave him the name which is above all other names; [10] so that all beings in the heavens, on earth and in the underworld, should bend the knee at the name of Jesus [11] and that every tongue should acknowledge Jesus Christ as Lord, to the glory of God the Father.

Rest

Contemplation is not some esoteric experience but simply a profound relationship with God. Friendship or love involves two people and a deep relationship cannot be forced where it does not exist. Only God can bring us to intimacy with God but we can prepare for this moment and we must respond to the invitation to intimacy when it comes. Trying to put the Gospel into practice each day is the best preparation but we cannot arrive at sanctity by dint of our own power. All is grace.

We can learn much from the saints who have gone before us. Saint Thérèse of Lisieux can be a great help. For her, trust was vital on the spiritual journey. Saint Thérèse wanted to respond fully to God, whom she believed to be calling her to holiness. However she realised that she lacked the strength. She was too weak to get to the summit of Mount Carmel and she could only admire the great saints from afar, knowing that it was impossible for her to imitate the works of these heroes of the faith.

Saint Thérèse had the profound intuition that all she had to do was to entrust herself completely to God, who alone could make her holy. Entrusting oneself to another is not easy, but for the path of contemplation, trust is essential because often we cannot see where we are going. Everyone is called to holiness but this vocation must be incarnated in the reality of each individual life. Saint Thérèse understood that she could not possibly become like the great saints but in fact she is now one of the most important saints in the history of the Church because of what she has to teach us, and certainly one of the most popular. Thérèse Martin responded to her vocation by dedicating her whole life to God in the enclosed monastery in Lisieux. She responded to the particular situation that she found in the monastery, being well aware that she could never respond totally to the love of God with her own strength, and so she entrusted herself whole heartedly into the hands of God.

Saint Thérèse of the Child Jesus, in a letter to a priest who had been entrusted to her as a "spiritual brother", wrote the following:

> When I see Magdalene come forward in face of the crowd of guests, and water with her tears the feet of her adored Master as she touches Him for the first time, I feel that her heart realised the fathomless depths of love and mercy in the Heart of Jesus, realised, despite her sins, that that Heart was ready not only to pardon her but actually to lavish on her the treasures of His divine intimacy and raise her to the highest summits of contemplation.[34]

It is not easy to lose control in any situation, including our personal relationships. Often the words we use in our prayers do not correspond with reality. It is only gradually we can learn to trust God. When our prayer begins to become more

---

34 Letter CCXX to Abbé Bellière in *Collected Letters of St. Thérèse of Lisieux*, (Sheed & Ward, London, 1949, 1977, 1979), pp. 306-307.

silent, we can have the sensation that we are doing nothing, and that we are actually going backwards, but we must have faith that God is at work within us. We must quieten not only the exterior noise but also the interior noise so that we can receive what God wants to give us.

I suggest entering into a period of silence now and, if you wish, there is the method of the *prayer of silence*, or prayer in secret, in the first Appendix, to help you.

Act

Here are some phrases from the text of Scripture that might help you to remember the presence of God throughout the day:

"man of God"

"he fell on his knees"

"he pleaded with him"

"the angel of Yahweh"

"do not be afraid"

The third captain who was sent to arrest Elijah had a great respect for the prophet of God and he approached him with humility. This reminds us of the importance of the biblical idea of fear of the Lord. Remember that fear of the Lord means having reverence toward God, who is our Creator and our Father. We must never take the grace of God for granted but seek to respond today to what we discern God is asking of us. We have only today to do the will of God.

Lord, for tomorrow and it's needs, I do not pray.
Give me your grace today that I might do your will.

Is there something that you have thought of doing for God or another person but never found the time to do? Why not do it today?

A window depicting the ascent of Elijah,
by Lavers & Barraud in the Stained Glass Museum, Ely.

Reflection 15
THE PROPHET ELIJAH RETURNS TO GOD
2 Kings **2:1-13**

Invocation

O God, your prophet Elijah appeared mysteriously without introduction and disappeared from the world in a fiery chariot. Elijah remains your servant forever. Help me to serve you as you desire and one day to leave this world to live with you. Through Christ our Lord. Amen.

Text

Read attentively the following text to capture the sense and to grasp the basic facts of the story:

[1] This is what happened when Yahweh took Elijah up to heaven in the whirlwind: Elijah and Elisha set out from Gilgal, [2] and Elijah said to Elisha, 'You stay here, for Yahweh is only sending me to Bethel.' But Elisha replied, 'As Yahweh lives and as you yourself live, I will not leave you!' and they went down to Bethel. [3] The brotherhood of prophets living at Bethel came out to meet Elisha and said, 'Do you know that Yahweh will carry your lord and master away today?' 'Yes, I know,' he said, 'be quiet.' [4] Elijah said, 'Elisha, you stay here, Yahweh is only sending me to Jericho.' But he replied, 'As Yahweh lives and as you yourself live, I will not leave you!' and they went on to Jericho. [5] The brotherhood of prophets living at Jericho went up to Elisha and said, 'Do you know that Yahweh will carry your lord and master away today?' 'Yes, I know,' he said, 'be quiet.' [6] Elijah said, 'Elisha, you stay here, Yahweh is only sending me to the Jordan.' But he replied, 'As Yahweh lives and as you yourself live, I will not leave you!' And they went on together. [7] Fifty of the brotherhood of prophets followed them, halting some distance away as the two of them stood beside the Jordan. [8] Elijah took his cloak, rolled it up and struck the water; and the water divided to left and right, and the two of them crossed over dry-shod. [9] When they

had crossed, Elijah said to Elisha, 'Make your request. What can I do for you before I am snatched away from you?' Elisha answered, 'Let me inherit a double share of your spirit.' [10] 'Your request is difficult,' Elijah said. 'If you see me while I am being snatched away from you, it will be as you ask; if not, it will not be so.' [11] Now as they walked on, talking as they went, a chariot of fire appeared and horses of fire coming between the two of them; and Elijah went up to heaven in the whirlwind. [12] Elisha saw it, and shouted, 'My father! My father! Chariot of Israel and its chargers!' Then he lost sight of him, and taking hold of his own clothes he tore them in half. [13] He picked up Elijah's cloak which had fallen, and went back and stood on the bank of the Jordan.

Read

Elisha wanted a double portion of Elijah's spirit. The double portion of an inheritance was traditionally the portion of the eldest son (*Deuteronomy* 12:17). Elisha wanted to be recognised as the legitimate successor to Elijah. In verse 12, Elisha expresses respect and dependence when he cries out, "My Father, my Father". In Elijah's days, Yahweh was considered as the God of life but not of death and so the dead were outside of Yahweh's sphere of influence. The ascension of Elijah was one of the few examples in the Bible where death was defeated. Centuries after, faith in the resurrection developed from examples such as this. The people always believed that Elijah would return (see *Mark* 6:5, 8:28). He disappeared but did not die, and so this was not a case of being raised from the dead. The people believed, and the Jews today still believe, that Elijah will return to announce the coming of the messiah.

Elisha is a witness to the miraculous departure of the prophet Elijah from the world. The goal of this account is to show that only Elisha among all the "sons of the prophets" was very close to Elijah and became his spiritual successor. This story was intended to fill the gap in knowledge regarding the end of the prophet Elijah and the site of his burial.

Reflect

Read the text again to hear what God is saying to you. To help you reflect on the text, there follows some questions. There is no right or wrong answer. There is only your answer to the Word of God, and this response must be lived on a daily basis.

1. What do you feel about death?

2. Do you have someone to accompany you on the spiritual journey?

3. Elisha requested a double portion of Elijah's spirit. What do you want to ask of God?

Respond

Elijah called Elisha to follow him and Elisha became a prophet after his master. Then Elisha became the leader of a group of prophets, dedicated to the true God. Jesus Christ has called us to follow him. Perhaps we will only discover gradually what God wants of us. In life we are faced with making many decisions. Every choice has certain consequences. Let us pray that our choices may be according to God's will.

> [18] As Jesus was walking by the Lake of Galilee he saw two brothers, Simon, who was called Peter, and his brother Andrew; they were making a cast into the lake with their net, for they were fishermen. [19] And he said to them, 'Come after me and I will make you fishers of people.' [20] And at once they left their nets and followed him. [21] Going on from there he saw another pair of brothers, James son of Zebedee and his brother John; they were in their boat with their father Zebedee, mending their nets, and he called them. [22] And at once, leaving the boat and their father, they followed him. (*Matthew* 4:18-22).

Rest

The prophet Elijah was always faithful to God but he did not always find it easy to be faithful. In this text, Elijah faces his own end. For us, remaining faithful to God is not, and will not, always be without difficulties, and we too must confront our own mortality.

Gradually on the contemplative path we are transformed but normally transformation does not seem to be the royal road to glory. Our human ways must be transformed to become divine ways of being but on this journey it can seem that we are losing everything.

> [54] And after this perishable nature has put on imperishability and this mortal nature has put on immortality, then will the words of

scripture come true: Death is swallowed up in victory. [55] Death, where is your victory? Death, where is your sting? [56] The sting of death is sin, and the power of sin comes from the Law. [57] Thank God, then, for giving us the victory through Jesus Christ our Lord. [58] So, my dear brothers, keep firm and immovable, always abounding in energy for the Lord's work, being sure that in the Lord none of your labours is wasted. (*1 Corinthians* 15:54-58)

I have already mentioned the concept of the *dark night*, which is a complex term for the process of transformation in those moments experienced as negative, or at least when everything is not clear. I would say that the dark night is the normal state for the greater part of life. The sensation of obscurity is sometimes greater and sometimes less. During the various phases of the transformation process we must pass through death, which, on this side of the grave, appears very dark for us. Throughout the course of our life, we must accept little deaths often in preparation for the end of our earthly existence. The first death is when we turn our backs on grave sin. We can be full of enthusiasm at this point on the spiritual journey but, contrary to what we may feel, we are still very far from perfection. We find that there is a long road still to travel.

As we continue our spiritual path, we become more mature and more ready to accept the little mortifications that are an essential part of the road to God. These mortifications are not necessarily works of penance that we ourselves choose but rather simply the difficulties of life. Gradually we see that our motivation is not totally pure, and we meet the *false self*, not in other people, but in ourselves. An increasing sensitivity to the presence of God makes us more sensitive to the action of the false self within us. We become more aware of the noise of our "internal compact disk" (all the comments about other people or on things that happen to us which go on within us during the day). A gradual detachment from these commentaries and from the operation of the false self is another experience of death. It is far from easy to accept that our motivation is not totally Christian. A profound humility is required and also a deep desire to be transformed.

By means of prayer, as a constant seeking of the face of God through all the ups and downs of life, we become more ready to let go of our own ideas of God in order to receive what God wishes to share with us. This process is yet again a kind of death. Finally we lose our own life in order to receive true life in abundance.

For the spiritual journey, faith is an absolute necessity. Faith first of all is a commitment towards the person of God whom we can neither see nor feel. It is a leap into the dark, trusting that there is Someone out there who loves us.

Often our personal prayer changes as we mature. What may help us at one phase may not be of help at another time. Prayer can become more simple while at the same time becoming darker. Whatever way you pray, trust in God and seek to respond to God's initiative in calling you to share an intimate relationship in the life of the Blessed Trinity.

Pray now as you can. There is the method in the first Appendix that perhaps could help you wait in silence for God, who is always present to us but whom we often experience as absent and as darkness. Consent to the presence of God in whatever way God chooses to come to you, and also to the divine purifying and transforming action.

Act

Here are some phrases from the text. Choose one or two to repeat now and again throughout the day to remind yourself of the presence of God. Naturally you will have your own little ways of keeping your relationship with God burning brightly. Any method is good if it helps you to remember the loving presence of God.

"took Elijah up to heaven"

"You stay here"

"Be quiet"

"I will not leave you"

"Make your request"

"Elijah went up to heaven"

"My father"

With this text we have arrived at the end of the prophet Elijah's life. He was always faithful to God and this fidelity cost him a great deal. The story of Elijah's departure from the earth left a profound impact on the religious memory of the Jews, but also on Christians and Muslims. The idea grew up that the prophet did not die and would return. We have already seen this idea in the New Testament (cf. *Matthew* 11:14).

Death is a mystery. We are followers of Jesus Christ who underwent death and was raised in the glory of the Father by the power of the Holy Spirit. When Christ appeared to his friends and disciples after his resurrection, it does not seem that he revealed everything that happens in the process of death and after death. However, Jesus is our leader (*Acts* 5:31; *Hebrews* 2:10). Christ came back from the dead and promised that we would go to be with him (*John* 14:3).

We must leave the future in the hands of God who loves us, and seek simply to remain faithful to God just like the prophet Elijah.

> We teach what scripture calls: *the things that no eye has seen and no ear has heard, things beyond the mind of man, all that God has prepared for those who love him.* (*1 Corinthians* 2:9).

*A window depicting the prophet Elijah rising to paradise in a fiery chariot,
by Marianne Behle-Downs, in Christ Church, Pompton Lakes, New Jersey.*

Appendix I
<u>PRAYER IN SECRET</u>

Lectio Divina is the most traditional way of growing in an intimate relationship with God and it is through this relationship that we are transformed and made capable of living Gospel in all its fullness. A monk of the 12th century has described the key moments of *Lectio Divina*: read the Word; reflect on the Word (meditate); respond to the Word (prayer during which we allow our hearts to spontaneously turn towards God); and rest in the Word (contemplation). The key moments are not rigid points to be followed one after the other but are descriptions of the way prayer normally develops, with one flowing into the other. There are some methods to help us when we begin to experience that all our words and thoughts are no longer sufficient. We may feel a call to silence but we do not know what to do.

I want to propose a method of prayer which can make silence very fruitful and can help us wait for God in silence. It is a method of Christian prayer that is based on the very rich contemplative tradition and especially on a classic book of this tradition called *The Cloud of Unknowing* written anonymously in the 14th century.[35] I am not suggesting that one should leave other personal ways of prayer, but this method could deepen these other methods and make them even more fruitful. The most important thing for this way of prayer is to be convinced that God is not far away but is very close. God is at home within us (cf. *John* 14:23).

This method of prayer is usually called *Centering Prayer* but could also be called the *prayer of silence* or the *prayer of desire* because in the silence we stretch out towards God with our desire.[36] It has also been called *prayer in secret*, following Jesus' counsel to go into one's private room and to pray to the Father in secret (*Matthew* 6:6).[37]

---

35 *Cloud of Unknowing and Other Works,* translated by Clifton Wolters, (London: Penguin Books, 1961).

36 Centering Prayer was taught originally by three Trappist monks in the U.S.A. who had made a profound study of the Christian contemplative tradition. Fr. Basil Pennington has written many books, such as *Centering Prayer* (London / New York / Sydney: Image Book, Doubleday, 1980). Fr. William Menninger has concentrated more on *The Cloud of Unknowing*; see his *The Loving Search for God* (New York: Continuum, 1994). The basic book to learn more about this way of prayer remains that of Fr. Thomas Keating, *Open Mind, Open Heart* (Massachusetts: Element Books, 1992). For a simple introduction to Centering Prayer and its background see Elizabeth Smith & Joseph Chalmers, *A Deeper Love*, (Tunbridge Wells, Kent: Burns & Oates, and New York: Continuum, 1999).

37 See the latest book by Thomas Keating, *Manifesting God*, (New York: Lantern Books, 2005).

The first phase of this prayer is to find a suitable place where the interruptions will be reduced to a minimum. Then get into a comfortable position that you can hold without fidgeting for the whole time of the prayer. Usually a minimum of 20 minutes is recommended.

One can begin this prayer with a short reading from the Bible. Now is not the time to think about the meaning of the words; that kind of meditation is for another time. Now is the time simply to be in the presence of God and consent to the divine action with our intention. Then, with eyes closed, introduce very gently a sacred word into your heart. A sacred word is a word that is very significant for you in your ongoing relationship with God. For example, the little word "yes" can mean a lot of things. "Do you want an ice cream?" "Yes". Or "Will you marry me?" "Yes". Such a little word can mean very little or a great deal and can change the whole of your life. In a close relationship two people can use pet-names for each other that may sound rather silly to outsiders but are highly significant to those involved in the relationship. The sacred word, then, should be sacred for you. According to the teaching of *The Cloud of Unknowing* it is better if this word be very brief, one syllable if possible.[38] I can suggest some possible words:

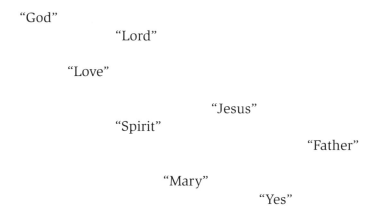

Choose a word that is most significant for you. Perhaps one will come to you if you ask God's help.

When I said to introduce the sacred word into your heart, I am not suggesting that you pronounce it with your lips or even mentally, but rather welcome it within you without thinking of its meaning. It is not necessary to force the sacred

---

38 *Cloud of Unknowing* (op. cit.) chapter 7, p. 69.

word. It should be very gentle. The sacred word is not a mantra to be constantly repeated. The word focuses our desire and we use it always in the same way simply to return our heart to the Lord as soon as we become aware that we are distracted. This is a prayer of *intention* and not *attention*. Our intention is to be in the presence of God and to consent to the divine action in our lives. The sacred word expresses this intention, and so when we become aware that we are thinking of something else we can decide either to continue with the distraction because we find it more interesting or return to our intention to be in the presence of God and consent to what God wants to accomplish in us. We return our heart to God by the very gentle use of the sacred word. It is a symbol of our intention. It is not necessary to repeat it frequently but only when we wish to return our heart to God.

During this prayer it is not the time to talk to God with beautiful words or even to have holy thoughts, even if we think that these are inspirations from God. These things are best left for another moment. Our silence and our desire are worth far more than many words.

By means of the word that we have chosen, we express our desire and our intention to remain in the presence of God and to consent to the purifying and transforming divine action. We return to the sacred word, which is the symbol of our intention and our desire, only when we become aware that we are involved in something else. The prayer consists simply in being in the presence of God without thinking of anything in particular. It is a prayer of relationship with God – Father, Son and Holy Spirit. If you understand how to be in silence with another person without thinking or doing anything in particular, then you will be able to understand what this prayer is all about. This method of prayer is not for everyone. If you feel an interior call to greater silence, it may be of help to you.

At the end of the period that you have decided to dedicate to prayer, perhaps you can say an *Our Father* or other prayer very slowly. It is good to remain in silence for a few moments in order to prepare yourself to bring the fruit of your prayer into your daily life.

Let's summarise the simple steps for this method of prayer.

Practical guidelines for Centering Prayer or the Prayer in Secret

There are four simple guidelines to this method of prayer.[39]

1. Choose a sacred word as the symbol of your intention to consent to the presence and action of God within.

2. Sitting comfortably and with eyes closed, settle briefly and then silently introduce the sacred word as the symbol of your consent to God's presence and action within.

3. When engaged with your thoughts, return ever so gently to the sacred word.

4. At the end of the prayer period, remain in silence with eyes closed for a couple of minutes.

---

39 See Thomas Keating, *Manifesting God,* pp. 133-139.

*Jesus Christ with his mother Mary, filled with the Holy Spirit,
standing before Carmel, the mountain of Elijah. Window by George Walsh
in the Chapel of Avila Discalced Carmelite Friary, Dublin.*

Appendix II
TEXTS IN THE OLD AND NEW TESTAMENTS
THAT MENTION THE PROPHET ELIJAH

Here follow the biblical texts that mention Elijah, with the exception of those treated at length in this book.

2 Kings 3:11
But the king of Judah said, "Is there no prophet of Yahweh here for us to consult Yahweh through him?" One of the king of Israel's servants answered, 'Elisha son of Shaphat is here, who used to pour water on the hands of **Elijah**'.

2 Kings 9:36
They came back and told Jehu, who said, 'This is the word of Yahweh which he spoke through his servant **Elijah** the Tishbite, "The dogs will eat the flesh of Jezebel in the field of Jezreel..." '.

2 Chronicles 21:12-15
Something written by the prophet **Elijah** then came into his hands. It said, 'Yahweh, God of your ancestor David, says this, "Since you have not followed the example of your father Jehoshaphat or of Asa king of Judah, [13] but have followed the example of the kings of Israel and have led Judah and the citizens of Jerusalem into apostasy, just as the House of Ahab has led Israel into apostasy, and have even murdered your brothers, your own family, who were better men than you, [14] Yahweh is going to afflict your people, your sons, your wives and all your property with a great calamity, [15] and you yourself with a severe disease affecting your bowels, as a result of which disease, continuing day after day, you will suffer protrusion of your bowels." '

1 Maccabees 2:58
Elijah for his consuming fervour for the Law was caught up to heaven itself.

Sirach (Ecclesiasticus) 48:1-12

Then the prophet **Elijah** arose like a fire, his word flaring like a torch. [2] It was he who brought famine on them and decimated them in his zeal. [3] By the word of the Lord he shut up the heavens, three times also he brought down fire. [4] How glorious you were in your miracles, **Elijah**! Has anyone reason to boast as you have? – [5] rousing a corpse from death, from Sheol, by the word of the Most High; [6] dragging kings down to destruction, and high dignitaries from their beds; [7] hearing a rebuke on Sinai and decrees of punishment on Horeb; [8] anointing kings as avengers, and prophets to succeed you; [9] taken up in the whirlwind of fire, in a chariot with fiery horses; [10] designated in the prophecies of doom to allay God's wrath before the fury breaks, to turn the hearts of fathers towards their children, and to restore the tribes of Jacob. [11] Blessed, those who will see you, and those who have fallen asleep in love; for we too shall certainly have life. [12] Such was **Elijah**, who was enveloped in a whirlwind; and Elisha was filled with his spirit; throughout his life no ruler could shake him, and no one could subdue him.

Malachi 3:23-24

'Look, I shall send you the prophet **Elijah** before the great and awesome day of Yahweh comes. [24] He will reconcile parents to their children and children to their parents, to forestall my putting the country under the curse of destruction.'

Matthew 11:12-14

Since John the Baptist came, up to this present time, the kingdom of Heaven has been subjected to violence and the violent are taking it by storm. [13] Because it was towards John that all the prophecies of the prophets and of the Law were leading; [14] and he, if you will believe me, is the **Elijah** who was to return.

Matthew 16:13-14

When Jesus came to the region of Caesarea Philippi he put this question to his disciples, 'Who do people say the Son of man is?' [14] And they said, 'Some say John the Baptist, some **Elijah**, and others Jeremiah or one of the prophets.'

Matthew 17:3-12

And suddenly Moses and **Elijah** appeared to them; they were talking with Jesus. [4] Then Peter spoke to Jesus. 'Lord,' he said, 'it is wonderful for us to be here; if you want me to, I will make three shelters here, one for you, one for Moses and one for **Elijah**.' [5] He was still speaking when suddenly a bright cloud covered them with shadow, and suddenly from the cloud there came a voice which said, 'This is my Son, the Beloved; he enjoys my favour. Listen to him.' [6] When they heard this, the disciples fell on their faces, overcome with fear. [7] But Jesus came up and touched them, saying, 'Stand up, do not be afraid.' [8] And when they raised their eyes they saw no one but Jesus. [9] As they came down from the mountain Jesus gave them this order, 'Tell no one about this vision until the Son of man has risen from the dead.' [10] And the disciples put this question to him, 'Why then do the scribes say that Elijah must come first?' [11] He replied, 'Elijah is indeed coming, and he will set everything right again; [12] however, I tell you that **Elijah** has come already and they did not recognise him but treated him as they pleased; and the Son of man will suffer similarly at their hands.'

Matthew 27:46-49

And about the ninth hour, Jesus cried out in a loud voice, 'Eli, eli, lama sabachthani?', that is, 'My God, my God, why have you forsaken me?' [47] When some of those who stood there heard this, they said, 'The man is calling on **Elijah**,' [48] and one of them quickly ran to get a sponge which he filled with vinegar and, putting it on a reed, gave it him to drink. [49] But the rest of them said, 'Wait! And see if **Elijah** will come to save him.'

Mark 6:14-15

King Herod had heard about Jesus, since by now his name was well known. Some were saying, 'John the Baptist has risen from the dead, and that is why miraculous powers are at work in him.' [15] Others said, 'He is **Elijah**,' others again, 'He is a prophet, like the prophets we used to have.'

Mark 8:27-28

Jesus and his disciples left for the villages round Caesarea Philippi. On the way he put this question to his disciples, 'Who do people say I am?' [28] And they told him, 'John the Baptist, others **Elijah**, others again, one of the prophets.'

Mark 9:4-13

Elijah appeared to them with Moses; and they were talking to Jesus. [5] Then Peter spoke to Jesus, 'Rabbi,' he said, 'it is wonderful for us to be here; so let us make three shelters, one for you, one for Moses and one for **Elijah**.' [6] He did not know what to say; they were so frightened. [7] And a cloud came, covering them in shadow; and from the cloud there came a voice, 'This is my Son, the Beloved. Listen to him.' [8] Then suddenly, when they looked round, they saw no one with them any more but only Jesus. [9] As they were coming down from the mountain he warned them to tell no one what they had seen, until after the Son of man had risen from the dead. [10] They observed the warning faithfully, though among themselves they discussed what 'rising from the dead' could mean. [11] And they put this question to him, 'Why do the scribes say that **Elijah** must come first?' [12] He said to them, '**Elijah** is indeed first coming to set everything right again; yet how is it that the scriptures say about the Son of man that he must suffer grievously and be treated with contempt? [13] But I tell you that **Elijah** has come and they have treated him as they pleased, just as the scriptures say about him.'

Mark 15:34-36
And at the ninth hour Jesus cried out in a loud voice, 'Eloi, eloi, lama sabachthani?' which means, 'My God, my God, why have you forsaken me?' [35] When some of those who stood by heard this, they said, 'Listen, he is calling on **Elijah**.' [36] Someone ran and soaked a sponge in vinegar and, putting it on a reed, gave it to him to drink saying, 'Wait! And see if **Elijah** will come to take him down.'

Luke 1:17
'With the spirit and power of **Elijah**, he will go before him to reconcile fathers to their children and the disobedient to the good sense of the upright, preparing for the Lord a people fit for him.'

Luke 4:25-26
'There were many widows in Israel, I can assure you, in **Elijah's** day, when heaven remained shut for three years and six months and a great famine raged throughout the land, [26] but **Elijah** was not sent to any one of these: he was sent to a widow at Zarephath, a town in Sidonia.'

Luke 9:7-8
Meanwhile Herod the tetrarch had heard about all that was going on; and he was puzzled, because some people were saying that John had risen from the dead, [8] others that **Elijah** had reappeared, still others that one of the ancient prophets had come back to life.

Luke 9:18-19

Now it happened that he was praying alone, and his disciples came to him and he put this question to them, 'Who do the crowds say I am?' ¹⁹ And they answered, 'Some say John the Baptist; others **Elijah**; others again one of the ancient prophets come back to life.'

Luke 9:29-33

And it happened that, as he was praying, the aspect of his face was changed and his clothing became sparkling white. ³⁰ And suddenly there were two men talking to him; they were Moses and **Elijah** ³¹ appearing in glory, and they were speaking of his passing which he was to accomplish in Jerusalem. ³² Peter and his companions were heavy with sleep, but they woke up and saw his glory and the two men standing with him. ³³ As these were leaving him, Peter said to Jesus, 'Master, it is wonderful for us to be here; so let us make three shelters, one for you, one for Moses and one for **Elijah**.' He did not know what he was saying.

John 1:19-25

This was the witness of John, when the Jews sent to him priests and Levites from Jerusalem to ask him, 'Who are you?' ²⁰ He declared, he did not deny but declared, 'I am not the Christ.' ²¹ So they asked, 'Then are you **Elijah**?' He replied, 'I am not.' 'Are you the Prophet?' He answered, 'No.' ²² So they said to him, 'Who are you? We must take back an answer to those who sent us. What have you to say about yourself?' ²³ So he said, 'I am, as Isaiah prophesied: A voice of one that cries in the desert: Prepare a way for the Lord. Make his paths straight!' ²⁴ Now those who had been sent were Pharisees, ²⁵ and they put this question to him, 'Why are you baptising if you are not the Christ, and not **Elijah**, and not the Prophet?'

Romans 11:2-4

God never abandoned his own people to whom, ages ago, he had given recognition. Do you not remember what scripture says about **Elijah** and how he made a complaint to God against Israel: ³ Lord, they have put your prophets to the sword, torn down your altars. I am the only one left, and now they want to kill me? ⁴ And what was the prophetic answer given? I have spared for myself seven thousand men that have not bent the knee to Baal.

James 5:17-18

Elijah was a human being as frail as ourselves – he prayed earnestly for it not to rain, and no rain fell for three and a half years; [18] then he prayed again and the sky gave rain and the earth gave crops.

The Carmelite Family in Britain

The Carmelite Order is one of the ancient religious orders of the Roman Catholic Church. Known officially as the *Brothers of the Blessed Virgin Mary of Mount Carmel*, the Order developed from a group of hermits in thirteenth-century Palestine; priests and lay people living a contemplative life modelled on the prophet Elijah and the Virgin Mary. By the year 1214 the Carmelites had received a *Way of Life* from Saint Albert, the Latin Patriarch of Jerusalem. Carmelites first came to Britain in 1242. The hermits became an order of mendicant friars following a General Chapter held in Aylesford, Kent, in 1247. Nuns, and lay men and women have always played a major part in the life of the Order, and have had formal participation since 1452. Over centuries of development and reform, the Carmelites have continued their distinctive mission of living 'in allegiance to Jesus Christ', by forming praying communities at the service of all God's people. The heart of the Carmelite vocation is contemplation, that is, pondering God and God's will in our lives.

Like the spirituality of all the major religious orders (Benedictines, Franciscans, etc.), Carmelite spirituality is a distinct preaching of the one Christian message. Carmelites blend prayerful contemplation with active service of those around them, and this takes many different forms depending on the time and the place they find themselves in. Over the centuries 'Carmel' has produced some of the greatest Christian thinkers, mystics, and philosophers, such as Teresa of Jesus (of Avila), John of the Cross, and Thérèse of Lisieux (three Carmelite 'Doctors of the Church'). In the twentieth century, the Carmelite Family bore witness to the Gospel in the martyrdoms of Titus Brandsma, Edith Stein, and Isidore Bakanja.

The British Isles boasted the largest Carmelite Province in the Order until its suppression at the Reformation. The British Province was re-established under the patronage of Our Lady of the Assumption in the twentieth century. There are communities of friars, sisters and lay Carmelites across England, Scotland, and Wales. Similar communities exist in Ireland, and throughout the world. The international Order of Discalced Carmelite friars, nuns, and laity is also present in Britain and Ireland. Members of the Carmelite and Discalced Carmelite Orders work, live, and pray together to make up the wider 'Carmelite Family', which seeks the face of the Living God in parishes, prisons, university chaplaincies, retreat centres, workplaces, schools, and through many other forms of ministry.

Further sources of information on Carmelite spirituality include:

John Welch, O.Carm.,
The Carmelite Way: An Ancient Path for Today's Pilgrim,
(Leominster: Gracewing, 1996).

Wilfrid McGreal, O.Carm.,
At the Fountain of Elijah: The Carmelite Tradition,
(London: Darton, Longman and Todd, 1999).

Website of the British Province of Carmelites
www.carmelite.org

Carmel on the web

The British Province of Carmelites
www.carmelite.org

Lay Carmel in Britain
www.laycarmel.org

Aylesford Priory, Kent
www.thefriars.org.uk

National Shrine of Saint Jude, Faversham
www.stjudeshrine.org.uk

Corpus Christi Carmelite Sisters
www.corpuschristicarmelites.org

Discalced Carmelite Family in England, Scotland & Wales
www.carmelite.org.uk

Irish Province of Carmelites
www.carmelites.ie

Anglo-Irish Province of Discalced Carmelites
www.ocd.ie

Thicket Priory, York
www.carmelite.org/thicket

Carmelite Forum of Britain and Ireland
www.carmeliteforum.org

Carmelite Institute of Britain and Ireland
www.cibi.ie

International Carmelite Index
www.carmelites.info

The Carmelite General Curia
www.ocarm.org

CITOC – Carmelite Communications Office
www.carmelites.info/citoc

Carmelite N.G.O. at the United Nations
www.carmelites.info/ngo

Edizioni Carmelitane
www.carmelites.info/edizioni

Domus Carmelitana, Rome
www.domuscarmelitana.com

NOTES

Also available in the Carmelite Bible Meditations series

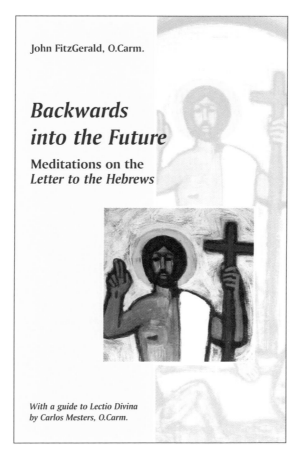

John FitzGerald, O.Carm.

Backwards into the Future

Meditations on the
Letter to the Hebrews

*With a guide to Lectio Divina
by Carlos Mesters, O.Carm.*

This and other titles on Carmelite spirituality and history can be ordered from:

The Friars Bookshop
The Friars
Aylesford
Kent
ME20 7BX
United Kingdom

☎ + 44 (01622) 715770

E-mail:
bookshop@thefriars.org.uk

Saint Albert's Press
Book Distribution
Carmelite Friars
P.O. Box 140
ME20 7SJ
United Kingdom

☎ + 44 (01795) 537038

E-mail:
saintalbertspress@carmelites.org.uk

Edizioni Carmelitane
Via Sforza Pallavicini, 10
00193 Roma
Italy

E-mail:
edizioni@ocarm.org

www.carmelite.org
www.carmelites.info/edizioni

LAUS DEO SEMPER ET MARIAE